W9-CDC-690

A Garland Series

The English Stage
Attack and Defense 1577 - 1730

A collection of 90 important works
reprinted in photo-facsimile in 50 volumes

edited by
Arthur Freeman
Boston University

Collier Tracts
1703-1708

with a preface
for the Garland Edition by

Arthur Freeman

Garland Publishing, Inc., New York & London

1973

Copyright © 1973

by Garland Publishing, Inc.

All Rights Reserved

Library of Congress Cataloging in Publication Data
Main entry under title:

Collier tracts, 1703-1708.

(The English stage: attack and defense, 1577-1730)
   Reprint of Mr. Collier's dissuasive from the
play-house, by Jeremy Collier, first printed in 1703,
for R. Sare, London; of The person of quality's answer
to Mr. Collier's letter, by John Dennis, first printed
in 1704 by the Booksellers of London and Westminster,
London; of A representation of the impiety & immorality
of the English stage (anonymous), first printed in 1704,
and sold by J. Nutt, London; of Some thoughts concerning
the stage (anonymous), first printed in 1704, and sold
by J. Nutt, London; of The stage-beaux toss'd in a

blanket, by Thomas Brown, first printed in 1704, and
sold by J. Nutt, London; and of A farther vindication of
the short view of the profaneness and immorality of
the English stage, by Jeremy Collier, first printed in
1708, for R. Sare, London.
   1. Theater--Moral and religious aspects.
I. Series.
PN2047.R4 1973   792'.013   70-170462
ISBN 0-8240-0618-6

Contents

Preface for This Edition.

v

Preface

After the spate of controversy, 1698-1700, which followed the initial provocation of Jeremy Collier's Immorality and Profaneness of the English Stage *(1698), peace settled on the press in this particular respect until 1703. At that date the so-called "second" Collier controversy began, and dragged on until 1708, whereupon new champions like Arthur Bedford, James Ralph, and William Law arose to assume the mantle abandoned by Collier himself. But a great thunderstorm which racked all England on 26-27 September 1703 proved too much of an incentive for the dormant Collier to ignore, and he followed it with a brief and redundant* Dissuasive from the Play-House . . . occasioned by the late Calamity of the Tempest, *probably the first theological exploitation of the disaster in theatrical terms, dated 10 December 1703, and published in time to be distributed* gratis *at church doors during the national fast day declared by Queen Anne for 19 June 1704. We*

7

PREFACE

reprint it (Lowe-Arnott-Robinson 294) from a copy in the possession of the publisher, collating A-B⁴.

Two other pamphlets were designed for similar dissemination. A Representation of the Impiety & Immorality of the English Stage *was attributed to Collier by Sister Rose Anthony, but his authorship is convincingly dismissed by Hooker; Maggs Brothers have cataloged a copy with the piquant contemporary holograph note, "19th Janry, Fast Day. This Book was given me at ye Church dore, and was distributed at most Churches." And yet* Some Thoughts concerning the Stage *(1704 as well) is more likely a production of Collier's pen, despite the odd assignation to Josiah Woodward by Halkett and Laing; Dennis (*The Person of Quality's Answer*) unequivocally calls it Collier's. We reprint* A Representation *from a copy in the British Museum (641.e.12[7]), collating A⁸B⁴, and* Some Thoughts *from the British Museum copy (641.e.46), collating A⁷ (Lowe-Arnott-Robinson 330 and 333).*

John Dennis wrote The Person of Quality's Answer to Mr. Collier's Letters *on or about 27 January in a white heat; it was advertised in the Term Catalogues from February 1704, and edited*

8

PREFACE

by Hooker (I, 299-319; notes, I, 501-5). We reprint a copy from Yale (Beinecke Hag 12 2 [vol. 5]), collating A^1B-E^4F^1 (Lowe-Arnott-Robinson 329).

The only reason for attributing The Stage-Beaux toss'd in a Blanket to Charles Gildon is found in a copy of Lowe's original bibliography now in the Folger Library, so annotated by Wilberforce (not "Wilbur") Eames, cited by Lowe-Arnott-Robinson, 335. The prologue and the epilogue alone contain specifically theatrical matter, but the play itself deals with "a pretending scourge to the English stage." Last of these tracts is Collier's own final fling at self-defense (1708, Lowe-Arnott-Robinson 297), rather after the fact, but occasioned by the entry into the ring of Edward Filmer, with his cogent Defence of Plays. We reprint The Stage-Beaux from the British Museum copy (643.i.18[8]), collating $A^1 a^4 B$-I^4, and Collier's A Further Vindication from the British Museum copy (1347.e.38), collating A-C^8.

May, 1973   A.F.

9

Mr. *COLLIER*'s
DISSUASIVE
FROM THE
PLAY - HOUSE;
IN A
LETTER
TO A
PERSON of QUALITY,

Occasion'd

By the late Calamity of the

TEMPEST.

LONDON:

Printed for RICHARD SARE, at *Grays-Inn-Gate* in *Holborn*. 1703.

SIR,

I Remember the laſt time I waited on you, you expreſs'd a very Chriſtian Concern at the Diſorders of the *Play-Houſe*, you lamented its having ſo much the Aſcendent of the *Town*, and the Countenance of *Figure* and *Fortune*. You ſeem'd to preſage that theſe Nurſeries of Licence and Atheiſm would, if unreſtrain'd, prove fatal to the Nation, make us ripe for Deſtruction, and pull down ſome terrible Vengeance upon our Heads. Being thus uneaſie in your Proſpect, and particularly ſolicitous for the Conduct of your Family and Relations, you were pleas'd to deſire me to draw up ſomething by way of Preſervative, in as narrow a Compaſs as poſſible. For, as you obſerve, in caſes of Conſcience and Morality, ſome People are ſo frightfully nice and impatient, that you muſt either cure them *extempore,* or not at all. The *Bill* muſt be ſhort, and the Medicine quickly ſwallow'd, or elſe they'll rather dye, than come under the Doctor.

Sir, waving other Reaſons of Regard for you, your Requeſt proceeds from ſo commendable a Motive, that upon this ſingle

Score

Score I think my self oblig'd to endeavour your Satisfaction.

And here give me leave to suggest to you, that having already in the *View* of the *Stage* spoken pretty largely to this Point, it will be impossible for me to pursue the Design without falling upon some of the Thoughts of that Performance: And since the Argument is thus forestall'd, your Candour, I question not, will make a proportionable Allowance.

To begin; The bad Complexion, and Danger of this Diversion, may be set forth,

First, From their representing Vice under Characters of Advantage. Dissolution of Manners is the great Favourite of the Modern *Muses*: To be thorough paced in that which is Ill, is the chief recommending Quality. A finish'd Libertine seldom fails of *View of* making his Fortune upon the *Stage*: Thus *the Immo-* qualified there is great Care taken to furnish *rality of* him with Breeding and Addreß: He is pre- *the Stage.* sently put into a Post of Honour, and an E- *Chap. 4.* quipage of Sense; and if he does the worst, *5, & alib.* he is pretty sure of speaking the best Things; I mean the most lively and entertaining. And all, to hold forth this profitable Instruction, (for so they must be interpreted) That Lewdness and Irreligion are the true Test of Quality,

lity, and Education. If a Man will be juſt
to the Intereſt of Reputation, he muſt throw
off the Reſtraints of Virtue, ſet up for a
Sceptick, and launch boldly into a Courſe of
Vice. For if he will be brow-beaten by the
other World, and over-aw'd by the Whim-
ſies of Conſcience, this is the Way to paſs for
a Clown, to taint his Blood, and almoſt
make him diſclaim'd at the *Herald*'s *Office*!
And that this wholeſom Doctrine may be the
better received, the Poets have taken care
to raiſe their *Ban* and *Arrier-Ban* upon all
that's Sacred and Solemn, and to perſecute
Virtue under every Appearance. And when
they make bold with a Character of Religion, they never fail of ſhewing it clumſey
and ridiculous. Such a Perſon muſt be an
Original in Untowardneſs, the Jeſt of the
Company, and put into all the Diſguiſes of
Folly and Contempt. And when Religion
is thus banter'd, and Virtue dreſs'd up in An-
tick, when Lewdneſs appears in Circumſtan-
ces of Credit, and makes ſuch a ſhining Figure; when Rewards and Puniſhments are
under ſo juſt a Diſtribution, the Government
of the *Stage* muſt needs be ſurprizingly regu-
lar, and improve the Audience to Admiration!

Secondly, Another Reaſon for the *Diſſua-*
ſive is the intolerable Profaneneſs of the
Stage. And here not to mention their Swearing

ing in all the Excesses of Distraction, and making bold with the Name of God on the most trivial and scandalous Occasions: This, tho' horrible enough, is the least Part of the Charge. Their Courage on this Head is of an amazing Size: They are Heroes beyond any thing upon Record, and in a manner perfectly new in their Defiance: They have attempted as it were to scale the Sky, and attack the Seat of Omnipotence: They have *View of* blasphem'd the Attributes of God, ridicul'd *the Stage.* his Providence, and burlesq'd the *old* and Chap. 2. *new* Testament. These infernal Sallyes put *and* 5. me in Mind of a late Instance of Resolution in one of their Fraternity; I mean the Man that acted *Jeptha's Rash Vow*, or the *Virgin Sacrifice* in *Smithfield*. The Subject of this Farce is taken out of the Book of *Judges*; and to peice up the Entertainment, and it may be to make the History ridiculous, there are several buffooning Characters tagg'd to the end on't. Now can there be a more irreligious Insolence than to mix the most solemn, and the most ridiculous Things together; to prostitute the inspired Writings in Places of Infamy, and to furnish out a Droll from the Sacred History. I hope it will be the last time the *Bible* will be shown for a *Sight* at *Bartholomew-Fair*.

I am unwilling to say any more upon this Matter: To suppose the Outrage of such

a

a Practice ftands in need of Satyr and Aggravation, is a Reflection upon the Common Senfe of a Nation, and looks as if we were blafted in our Underftandings.

Thirdly, The next thing I fhall remark is the Indecency of their Language: And here the Englifh Poets and *Players* are ftill like themfelves ; they ftrain to a Singularity of Coarnefs : The modern *Theatres* of *Europe* are meer *Veftals* to them : They outdo the Liberties of *Greece* and *Rome,* the Ages of Ignorance, and the Precedents of Heathenifm. The Lufcioufnefs of double Entendres, and remote Glances wont ferve their Turn : To flafh a little upon the Imagination, and appear in the Twylight, is not Mifchief enough ; No : They love to have their Senfe clear and determin'd : They labour for Perfpicuity, and fhine out in Meridian Scandal : They make the Defcription rank, bring the Images clofe, and fhow the Monfter in its full Proportions. And by this Stench the Spirits are infenfibly feiz'd, and the Health of the Company often fuffers. Thus the Impreffions of Modefty wear off, the Affections are debauch'd, and the Memory furnifh'd with Ammunition to play upon the Confcience. And is this Diverfion for Chriftians ? Is this fuitable to that Holinefs of Doctrine, to that Sobriety of Thought prefcrib'd by the Gofpel, or to that Tafte of Satisfaction we expect

View of Stage. Chap. 14

Ibid. & Chap. 5.

pe&

pect in the other World ? Can the Ladies be entertained with such Stuff as This ? Those that dress their Diet, would make us believe their Palates are strangely out of Order. To treat the Reservedness of their Sex, their Birth and their Breeding with Smut and Ribaldry, is, to speak softly, incomprehensible Manners. In short, it will be said, and therefore I shall put the Case ; *either the Ladies are pleased with the Indecencies of the Stage or they are not* : If they are, 'tis a hard Imputation on their Virtue : It argues they have strangely forgotten the Engagements of *Baptism*, the Maxims of Education; and the Regards of their Character. 'Tis a Sign they are strongly seiz'd by the Infection, and that the *Tokens* are almost ready to break out. *If they are not pleased*, 'twill be enquired why they come there ? Why they venture upon a Place where they must expect to have their Imagination shock'd, their Aversion put into a Fit, and their Blood call'd up into their Faces ? Who would undergo so much Fatigue of Fancy and Mortification ? The *Play-House* is without Doubt the wrong Place for Discipline ; And such Pennance if often repeated will never pass for good Earnest. Thus the Dilemma bears hard towards the Ladies : And for my Part, I confess, I have not Logick enough to disengage them.

Fourthly,

Fourthly, We muſt not forget the Incorrigibleneſs of the *Stage*; This is a farther Aggravation of their Diſorder: Their ill Plays have been ſome of them examin'd, their licentious Extravagance mark'd, and repeated Inſtances produced upon them. In ſhort, the Ulcer has been diſſected, the Criminals dragg'd out, and the Blaſphemy expos'd. The *View the S* Poets, tis true, rallyed upon the Defeat, and made the moſt of their Matters. But finding the Cauſe too groſs and defenceleſs, and that the Force of Truth would prevail; they have ſince lay'd down, and left the *Field* But this is not all; The *Players* have met with farther Inſtruction: The *Laws* have been let looſe upon them; They have been diſciplin'd at *Weſtminſter-Hall*. However, all this Conviction and Diſcouragement wont do. They areProof againſt Reaſon and Puniſhment, againſt *Fines* and Arguments, and come over again with their old Smut and Profaneneſs. One would think by their deſperate Puſhing, they were reſolv'd to exterminate Religion, and ſubdue the Conſcience of the Kingdom. And I muſt needs ſay, their Meaſures are not taken amiſs. They have without Doubt pitched upon the moſt likely Expedient to make Vice abſolute, and Atheiſm univerſal.

B   And

And as if the old *Batteries* were too weak, They have ftrengthened the Attack, and levyed *Recruits* of Mufick and Dancing beyond Sea. There was great Occafion, no Queftion, to draw down more Forces upon *Flefh* and *Blood* ; and to fpring a new Mine to help ftorm the Senfes, and blow up the Paffions to Combuftion! And when People are thus thrown off their Guard, and difarm'd of their Difcretion, the *Play-Houfe* is admirably furnifh'd with *Provifion* to feize the Advantage, and improve the Opportunity. For what is it but the common Receptacle of Vice, and the *Rendevouz* of Rakes and Strumpers ? I don't mean all the Company are fuch. But this I may fay, that fcarce any Quarter is fo plentifully ftock'd. Now who would truft his Health in a Place of Mortality, or go to the *Peft-Houfe* for Recreation ?

What then, muft we never fee a Play ? And where's the Harm on't if we don't ? Can't we take an ill Thing upon Report, without the Curiofity of Experience ? Is it not better to ftand off from unneceffary Danger, than to prefs upon a formidable Enemy, and run the Hazard of a Defeat ? However, if young People are fo uneafy at fuch a Reftraint ; if they will needs venture, let them fortifie themfelves at Home, and
take

take the Guard of Religion along with them:
Let them go, as they do, to fee an outlandifh
Monfter, once in their Life time : Let the
Play be, prefcribed them by Perfons of Con-
duct and Sobriety : In a Word, let the
Snake be frozen, and the Poifon as much di-
luted as 'tis poffible.

And after all, I don't pretend to give a Licence for feeing the *Play-Houfe*, though under the Cautions above-mention'd : But if
People will rufh forward, and ftand the E-
vent, I only defire to direct the Motion, and
fuggeft the fafeft Way.

Fifthly, The *Play-Houfe* has been look'd
on as a publick Nufance, cenfur'd and dif-
countenanc'd by *Church* and *State*, and that
in times both Ancient and Modern.

To give fome Inftances in the *State*.

The Republick of *Rome*, before *Julius Cæfar* ftopt the building of a Theater, being
fully convinc'd, that this Diverfion would
bring in foreign Vice, that the Old *Roman*
Virtue would be loft, and the Spirits of the
People emafculated. This wife Nation made
the Function of *Players* fcandalous, feiz'd
their Freedoms, and threw them out of Privilege and Reputation.

*Defenc,
of the
View, &.
p. 85.*

To

To come down to our own Conſtitution :
The *Players* are forbidden to Act, and ſcatter
their Infection through the Kingdom, under
very ſevere and infamous Penalties. And in
the Reign of the Famous Queen *Elizabeth*,
there was an Order of Queen and Council,
to drive the *Players* out of the City and Liberties of *London*, and to pull down the *Theaters*, which was executed accordingly. In
France ſome few Years ſince the *Italian
Players* were expell'd the Kingdom, and now
the *French* Stage lyes under Excommunica-
tion. The Theaters have been lately ſhut
up in *Italy* by the *Pope*, and in the Territories
of *Brandenburgh* by the King of *Pruſſia*. And
ſeveral *European* Countries would never endure them in any Form, or under any Regulation.

As to the *Church*, the *Players* ſtand condemn'd by ſeveral Councils of great Antiquity
and Credit. And the moſt Celebrated and
Primitive Fathers have declaimed loudly a-
gainſt the *Stage*, with all the Zeal, Force,
and Rhetorick imaginable. So that if the
ſtrongeſt Precedents, either in *Church* or *State*,
will make any Impreſſion upon us, if we
have any Regard for the Wiſdom and Piety
of the beſt and moſt conſiderable part of Mankind, if Authority will move us, if Reaſon
will convince us, if Experience will teach us,
we

*View of
the Stage,*
chap. 6.

39 Eliz.
cap. 4.

1 Jac.
cap. 7.

*View of
the Stage.*
chap. 6.

Ibid.

Ibid.

we have the ftrongeft Motives imaginable to ftand off from fuch dangerous Ground.

To this I may Obferve in the

Sixth Place, That fuch fcandalous Diverfion muft of Neceffity untune our Minds, and difpirit our Devotion. If the Stage once gains our Fancy, the Service of God will grow burthenfom and heavy. And when a lufcious Song becomes relifhing, a Pfalm will be a flat Entertainment. Is it poffible for Efteem and Contempt to ftand together, and can we reverence that which has been our Sport to fee defpifed? To fpend the Week at the *Play-Houfe*, and come to *Church* on the *Sunday*, looks little better than Fafhion and Grimace. Thefe two *Places* are ftrangely *hoftile* and counterqualifying: For what *Communion has Light with Darknefs,* *and what Concord has C H R I S T with Belial?* If we *fit thus in the Seat of the Scornful*, 'tis in vain to approach his Prefence, and *to tread his Courts.*

2 *Cor.* 6. 14, 15.

And therefore in the

Laft Place I fhall add, That to frequent the *Play-Houfe* is plainly inconfiftent with the Duties and Character of a Chriftian. For, not to repeat what has been faid, the Guilt of the Place muft in a great Meafure fall up-

on

on the *Audience*: To be prefent, after warning, at the Abufe of Religion, amounts to Confent and Approbation. To delight in ill Company, is to become part of it, and all People are *Principals* in Profanenefs, as well as in Murther. Every one knows 'tis the Company that fupports the *Play - Houfe.* Without a numerous Audience they would be forc'd to disband, to furrender their Bufinefs, and, it may be, be difcouraged into Reformation. What then? Are we to affift fuch Places of Liberty and Prophanenefs with our Purfe and Perfon? Muft we keep up the Credit of Debauchery? Muft we make a Contribution for Blafphemy, and raife a Tax for the Government *Below?* To countenance fuch Practices muft inevitably communicate the Guilt, and heighten the Provocation. And when Wickednefs is thus flaming and outragious, we cannot expect but that Vengeance will quickly follow,

We have lately felt a fad Inftance of God's Judgments in the terrible Tempeft: Terrible beyond any thing in that Kind in Memory, or Record. For not to enlarge on the lamentable Wrecks, and Ruins, were we not almoft fwept into a Chaos? Did not Nature feem to be in her laft Agony, and the World ready to expire? And if we go on ftill in fuch Sins of Defyance, may we not be afraid

of

of the Punifhment of *Sodom*, and that God fhould deftroy us with *Fire* and *Brimftone*.

What Impreffion this late Calamity has made upn the *Play-Houfe*, we may guefs by their Acting *Macbeth* with all its Thunder and Tempeft, the fame Day: Where at the mention of the *Chimnies being blown down*, (*Macbeth*, *p.* 20.) the *Audience* were pleas'd to *Clap*, at an unufual Length of Pleafure and Approbation. And is not the meaning of all this too intelligible? Does it not look as if they had a Mind to out-brave the Judgment? And make us believe the Storm was nothing but an Eruption of *Epicurus*'s Atoms, a Spring-Tide of Matter and Motion, and a blind Salley of Chance? This throwing Providence out of the Scheme, is an admirable *Opiate* for the Confcience! And when Recollection is laid afleep, the *Stage* will recover of Courfe, and go on with their Bufinefs effectually.

Thus, Sir, I have lay'd before you what I have to offer upon this Occafion, and am,

Your moft humble Servant.

December 10.
1703.

J. C.

F I N I S.

Books Printed for *Richard Sare*, at *Grays-Inn-Gate* in *Holbourn*.

The Devout Chriftian's Manual of Prayers and Devotions for all Occafions. Containing fpecial Litanies for *Sundays*, *Wednefdays*, and *Frydays*; alfo particular Offices for the Holy Communion, in the Time of Sicknefs, and for a Recovery, &c. Supervifed add Recommended by the Reverend Mr. *Wagftaff*.

An Anfwer to all the Excufes and Pretences which Men ordinarily make for their not coming to the Holy Communion, Price 3d. or 20. s. a Hundreds

Some fhort and plain Direftions for fpending one Day well, Price 1d. or 6. s. a Hundred.

Plain Inftruftions to the Young and Ignorant, Price 3d. or 20 s. a Hundred.

An Effay towards making the Knowledge of Religion eafie to the meaneft Capacity, Price 2d. or 12 s. a Hundred.

The Cannon of the New Teftament Vindicated, in anfwer to the Objeftions of J. Toland. By John Richardfon, B D. formerly Fellow of Emanuel Col. Camb. the 2d Edition.

The Chriftian Scholar, Price 3d. or 20 s. a Hundred.

THE
Perſon of Quality's
ANSWER
TO
Mr. COLLIER'S
LETTER,
BEING A
DISSWASIVE
FROM THE
PLAY-HOUSE.

In which are Inſerted the Apolo-
gies of a Young Lady, and Young Gentleman, in behalf of the Ladies and Gentlemen who frequent the Play-Houſe.

LONDON:
Printed and are to be Sold by the Bookſellers of *Lon
don* and *Weſtminſter.* 1 7 0 4.

THE

Perſon of Quality's

A N S W E R

TO

Mr. COLLIER's LETTER, &c.

Dear Doctor,   Lincolns-Inn-Fields,
Jan. the 27th.

THIS Afternoon, I received your Edifying, Evan-
gelical Diſſwaſive; for which, What thanks can I
return you? What recompence can be ſufficient?
May he, for whoſe ſake you did it, amply Reward you.

*I had conceived indeed a Zealous concern at the Diſorders
of the Play-Houſe, I lamented its having ſo much the aſcen-
dant of the Town, and the Countenance of Figure and Fortune. And I too juſtly preſaged that theſe Nurſeries of Li-
cenſe and Atheiſm, eſpecially that in our Neighbourhood, wou'd
if unreſtrain'd, prove fatal to the Nation;* make us Ripe for
*Deſtruction, and pull down ſome terrible Vengeance on our
Heads;* no leſs than Popery, or Arbitrary Power at the
leaſt, and dear Doctor, What a Day, and what a ſight
wou'd that be to you and me?

B   For

For this Reason I refolved that in my Family, Reformation and the Year fhould begin together, and for that Reafon I called them together as foon as they had dined to Day; determining to Read a long and a folemn Lecture out of your fhort view to them; but a ftrange fatality had happened, for fome audacious Rats had fo prophanely gnawn it, that it was no longer legible, a detachment in my Confcience of Play-Houfe Vermin, whom the Devil had enter'd into for that purpofe, at his Congregation in the Neighbourhood.

Thus bilk'd of my Homily, I thought I muft to my great Grief, have been forced to difmifs my Flock. For I perceived they were grown *frightfully Nice and Impatient, and were refolved to be cur'd extempore or not at all.*

But then it was that in an aufpicious Moment, arriv'd your fhort, but Divine Diffwafive. I read it over as it were in a Breath, while they all the while ftood gaping to entertain it. But the laft incomparable Paragraph but one, I pronounc'd with a more Emphatical Voice; Laid before them with all the Energy of my Lungs, *the faid inftance of God's Judgment in the Terrible Tempeft, when we were almoft fwept into Chaos,* when Nature *feem'd to be in her laft Agony, and the World feem'd ready to expire.* And what occafion faid I to my gaping Audience, to have recourfe to Tragedies, when thofe Rants, that Fuftian, and that Bombaft, with which deluded Mortals, are now a days fo tickled, are engagingly inferted into our very Diffwafives?

And here Doctor I made two Remarks to them, upon the Judgment of the late Dreadful Tempeft. For firft faid I, the outcries of the Play-Houfe practices are fo Aggravating, fo Horrible, that the Divine Vengeance which they brought down upon us, has involv'd the very Innocent. Not only the Poor Inhabitants of *Cologn*, but the very

very *Hamburghers* and *Dantzichers*, and all the People of the *Baltick*, have suffer'd for the Enormities of our *English* Theatres; tho' I believe in my Conscience they never so much as heard of a Play, and know no more the difference between a Tragedy and Comedy, than they do the distance between the Earth and Saturn; so that, said I, you may observe from hence, 'tis not enough to keep away from these lewd Entertainments; but you must endeavour with all your might to suppress the Conventicles of Satan.

The second Observation that I made was this, that we have reason to be thankful to Heaven, for forbearing us so long. For if the late Dreadful Judgment had happen'd in the Reign of King *Charles* the Second, when the Play-Houses were Licentious in all their Impunity, when Reformation was so far from being thought of, that the very name was despised and laugh'd at. What must the dismal Consequence not have been ? Then we should certainly have been swallow'd up ; since the *Judgment* was so terrible even the other Day, after a five Years Reformation ?

What reason have we to be thankful, that we live in an Age in which Light is come into the World. For in what *Ægyptian* darkness have we liv'd hitherto ? And what a poor Reformation was that which was carried on in Queen *Elizabeth*'s time, in Comparison of that which you are gloriously projecting ? For with that former Reformation the Play-House began ; grew up and spread and flourish'd. What a shadow of a Reformation was that ? 'Tis true Popery was driven out, and wholsome Laws were Enacted to secure the Rights of the Pople. But what signified all that when the Play-House was encourag'd ? For tho' as you learnedly observe, Play-Houses, in the Reign of that Great Queen, were not permitted to be erected in the Liberties of the City, yet in the Subburbs they were not only permitted but encourag'd with a Vengeance; and by whom

B 2   encourag'd ?

encourag'd ? Why not only by the People, but by the
Court, nay, by the Council, yes by thofe poor deluded
Wretches, *Cecil* anc *Walfingham*, who believ'd it to be the
bufinefs of forfooth Wife States-Men, to provide Honeft
and Reafonable Diverfions for the People ; and at the fame
time were fo infatuated, fo intoxicated, as to believe the
Entertainments of the Theatre, not only to be Honeft and
Reafonable, but the only Honeft and Reafonable Diverfions.

Nay the poor miftaken Queen her felf, encouraged Play-
Houfes to that degree, that fhe not only commanded
Shakefpear, to write the Comedy of the *Merry Wives*, and
to write it in Ten Days time; fo eager was fhe for the wicked
Diverfion ; but ev'n with that Hand that weilded the Scep-
ter defcended poorly to Tranflate a Play that was writ by
a *Grecian* Poet. She had read it feems of fome Great Men
among the *Romans*, who had fhewn the way ; As *Julius
Cæfar* had writ *Adraftus*, *Auguftus Ajax*, *Gracchus Thyeftes*,
and *Mecenas Octavia*, and fhe wanted Judgment, alas poor
Woman, to diftinguifh between the obligations of a Heathen and a Chriftian. 'Tis true fhe was Wife enough in
fome things, fhe kept out Popery and Arbitrary Power,
fhe defended us from *Rome* and *Spain*, by the meer Force
of her Prudence. But what fignified that, you know
Doctor, when fhe encourag'd the Play-Houfes, and wanted
fore-fight in that particular, to prefage that thefe Nurferies
of Vice and Atheifm would prove fatal to the Nation ?

It feems fome Fools about her had told her, that at a
time when Taxes were frequent and grievous, fome honeft
Diverfions would comfort the People, but that it would be
unreafonable to deprive them at once of their Money, and
of their Pleafure too ; this fhe had been told, and fhe like
an eafie Woman believ'd it. But what amazes me moft is
this Doctor, that not only that Queen and her Council encouraged Plays, but not fo much as one of the Famous Pre-
lates

lates in her time said so much as a word against them. 'Tis
true, the State-Men defended us against *Spain* very vigor-
ously, and very effectually, and so did the Church-Men
against the *Roman* See; but alas their poor and narrow
Spirits contented themselves with that. But not so much as
one word was said against the Abominations of the Play-
Houses. There were Reformers indeed! Were they so
senless that they wanted discernment to see the *flaming and
outragious wickedness* of them? Or so very wicked that
they wanted Zeal to discharge their Duty in the suppressing
it? Ah my dear Doctor, Had you but liv'd in those Times,
you would have taught that Queen her Lesson, in Loyal
Libels have told her her Duty, affronted her Authority, de-
fam'd her Servants, and boldly have told her that she Countenanc'd them only to Debauch her People. You would
have open'd the Eyes of those Fools, who believ'd *Shake-
spear* to be Instructive as well as Innocent. You would
have extracted more *Smutt* from his Comedies, than a
Chimney does from Seacoal. And what Prophaneness and
Blasphemy had you not found in his Tragedies? You
would have satisfied both Queen and Council, and Clergy
too, that their business was to suppress the Play-Houses,
and to let *Spain* and *Rome* alone. That the Danger that they
were in was not from *Philip* the Second, and *Sixtus* the Fifth;
but from Tyrants who had been many a Year defunct from
Julius Cæsar and *Macbeth*; you would have ·presaged· the
Storm that the latter would have pull'd down upon the
Nation, a Hundred Years after 'twas writ. You had then
been *Histrio Mastix* the first, whereas you are now but
the second of that glorious Name; and then had old
Bungling *Pryn* been cropt for presuming to Copy you.
Thus, my dear Doctor, we have reason to believe what you
would have done, from what we behold you do. For tho'
Popery and Slavery are at our Doors, and each moment
are rushing in upon us; and nothing but the Wisdom of one
Woman

Woman ſtands between us and them, yet you ſtill retain
your commendable Paſſive Principle, appear as unconcern'd
as if you had Sworn to be a Foe to neither, are found to
be as little alarm'd for the Church, as if you had thrown
off its Cauſe as you have caſt off its Habit; and inſtead of
crying out Slavery, Popery, do nothing but cry out the
Play-Houſe, the Play-Houſe, with as much Fury as if you
were afraid it ſhould contribute to the keeping them
out.

But my dear Doctor, By the leave of your Modeſty, I
muſt exalt your Glory to a higher pitch. When Queen
Elizabeth died King *James* ſucceeded him; and among the
Eminent Reformers of his Reign there was no talk of the
Stage. Nay, on the contrary, to their ſhame be it ſpoken,
that King and his Court appear'd to be infinitely delighted
with Plays. And in his Viſits to the two Univerſities,
Plays were the chief of his Entertainment. But what would
we have Doctor; as the Education is, ſo is the Youth.
And he had been tutor'd by old *George*, a Notorious Reformer, but a Notorious Playwright. For the Sot believ'd
it ſeems that the *Drama* could contribute to the Reformation of Mankind.

To King *James* ſucceeded King *Charles* the Firſt; and
then aroſe another Famous Reformer, *John Milton* by name,
who not only left a Tragedy behind him, the Story of
which he impiouſly borrow'd from the Bible, written to
leave him without excuſe in his mature, nay declining
Years, but has left a fine Encomium on *Shakeſpear*; has
ſhewn an extraordinary eſteem for *Johnſon*; and among all
the things that he thought fit to Reform, ſo far had pre-
judice laid hold of his Underſtanding, it never ſo much as
came into his Head that the Stage was one of them.

But then about that time, Doctor, there aroſe a Reformer
indeed, Brother *Pryn* of Illuſtrious Memory; a Perſon indeed of an *amazing* boldneſs. For to the fervency of his
Furious

Furious Spirit, Ruine and Reformation were all one. With these Zealot's Thoughts he set about Reforming the Church as well as the Stage; and by preparing the downfal of one made way for the Ruine of the other. 'Tis true, he lost some part of himself in the Cause. But happy the Ears that were so lost! How much happier than those that stand pricking up daily at the Ribaldry of our Modern Comedies? I know, dear Doctor, under the Rose, that you have the same Design, and that you will never leave off writing as long as there is left either a Prelate or Poet in *England*; or if you do condescend to admit of Bishops, you will at least suffer no such Bishops as have a Tang of the Stage, I mean no Swearing Prophane Bishops, but such whose Meek and Christian Communication is only Yea and Nay.

As you have the same noble Design, may you find better Fortune, as you well deserve. For he, my dear Doctor, was but a Type, of your more Excellent self, tho' indeed an Illustrious Type. And he but anticipated in a cold and gloomy way, the very things that Fate had designed to be said with Fire and Flame by you. He indeed overthrew but for a time the Church and Stage together. But may you with a more propitious Fate- -. But hold !--- No Man, you know is able to tell into whose hands a Letter may fall.

Thus, Doctor the blessed Work of Reformation went on; and down went the Bishops and the Stage together; but after they had lain for some time in the dust were restor'd together, and with them the banish'd King.

And there are not People wanting, who believe, that the Restoring the Stage, was one of the Motives to the Restoring the banish'd King, for say they, the People of *England* were at last grown weary of a Nasty, Gloomy, Sullen, Fanatical Government, and began to long for their Pleasures. How my dear Doctor? The restoring the

Stage

Stage was one of the Motives to reſtoring the baniſh'd King.
Ah my dear Doctor, if you had but flouriſh'd in that Au-
ſpicious Juncture; How happy would you have eſteem'd
your ſelf to have been the Inſtrument of ſuppreſſing the
Stage, only on purpoſe to ſee it reſtor'd with ſuch a Glorious Attendant.

Well! The King, the Biſhops and the Stage were re-
ſtored together, and a long time flouriſh'd together, without any talk of reforming the Play-Houſes, much leſs of
ſuppreſſing them. For the Merry Miniſters of that Happy
Prince laugh'd at a Reformation. And even the former
Miniſters of the Church at that time, among whom were
certainly ſome of the greateſt Men that the Chriſtian World
has produc'd ; appear'd by no means to be ſo terribly
alarm'd at the Entertainments of the Stage.

You your ſelf, I remember Doctor, were then at Years
of Diſcretion; and yet with Paſſive Ears and Tongue, en-
dur'd the Filth of *Epſom*-Wells, the Bawdy of the Soldier's
Fortune, and the Beaſtlineſs of *Limber-Ham*. But the time
of your Prophetick Miſſion it ſeems was not yet come, or
perhaps you thought it improper to fall out with the Play-
Houſes, before you had fallen out with the Government.
But you have at laſt, to the wonder of the World, declar'd
your ſelf, and we may ſay of you, what *Lucretius* ſaid of
his ador'd *Epicurus*, Pardon the Compariſon, I beſeech you
Doctor,

> *That you in Wit ſurpaſs Mankind as far,*
> *As does the Midday Sun, the Midnight Star.*

For what in the Beginning of the Reformation was never
ſeen, neither by *Jewell*, nor *Ridley*, nor *Cranmer*, nor *La-
timer* ; nor was afterwards hardly ſo much as thought of,
by the Judicious, the Penetrating, the Sagacious *Hooker* ;
nor what in this latter end of it, (as under the Roſe we
ſweetly

ſweetly hope Doctor) has not been found out neither by *Wilkins* nor *Tillotſon*, who have ſhown ſo
much Underſtanding and ſo much Judgment ; as well
by the force of their Invincible Arguments, as of
their Clear, Chaſte, Noble and Maſculine Styles ;
What none of theſe have been able to find , you
have.plainly convinc'd the World of ; that the Play-
Houſe would bring all to ruine ; O Miracle of
boundleſs Sagacity ! O Prodigy of Penetration !
The late Arch-Biſhop was certainly a Man of as undoubted Probity, of as much Integrity, as ever liv'd
in the World; nor was his Zeal and his Boldneſs in
the cauſe of Virtue leſs ; witneſs that Noble, that
Intrepid Spirit, with which he appear'd againſt Popery, even in the moſt Dangerous times, when the
Jeſuits us'd ſharp deciſive Arguments, and made nothing of cutting a Man's Throat out of Zeal to Con-
fute his Doctrine ; the late Archbiſhop, I ſay, Doctor,
who had ſo much Boldneſs, as well as Zeal and Integrity, and who in the late Reign had ſo much
Pow'r ; never ſaw this dreadful Danger from Plays,
which you have ſo plainly diſcover'd. * For if he had
ſeen it, he would have prevail'd upon the late Queen
to ſuppreſs them. He either foreſaw none of this
Danger, or if he did, the good miſtaken Man, thought
there would be more in going about to prevent it.
An infallible ſign that he wanted your fore-ſight and
your Sagacity. He look'd upon himſelf to be indi-
ſpenſably bound in a double reſpect to Reform the
Corruptions of the times. For he was both Head
of the Church, and firſt Couſellour of State. And
no Man knew better then that Judicious Prelate,
that Corruptions of Manners are moſt pernicious both
to Church and State. And no Man ever diſcover'd

the margin note: * There is ſomething in the E-leventh Volume of his Sermons a-gainſt Plays, which I had not ſeen when this was Writ; but Mr. Collier has prevarica-ted vilely in the Que-tation.

C   more

more Zeal for the prefent Eftablifhment, both in Church and State. And yet poor Man with all his Underftanding, and all his Zeal, he was fo far deluded in this particular, that he never medled with thefe Nurferies of Licenfe and Atheifm. As many admirable Sermons as he left behind him, againft the Vices and the Errors of the Times; I believe you will hardly find that he has mentioned the Play-Houfes with bitternefs in them all. He left that part of Reformation for your fublimer Prudence, and more Heroick Charity. Indeed the Concern that he had himfelf both in Church and State was fo apparent, that perhaps he might fear that a violent endeavour to Reform our Theatres in him might look like Intereft; and might perhaps imagine that the Work would be kindlier received, if it were carried on by one who cared not a Farthing either for Church or State.

And here Doctor give me leave to admire the Glory, or to fpeak in your own Diviner Language, the *Meridian blaze of your myfterious - Charity.* 'Tis of an *amazing fize and brightnefs,* and our weak Eyes are dazled at it. For that you dear Doctor, who appear fo extreamly Nice and Scrupulous, that you dare not fo much as take an Oath to defend our Sovereign Lady and us, againft our Mortal Enemies; you who are fo over cautious that you dare not fo much as hold any Communion with us, that you fhould take up this extream concern for our Souls, that you fhould be fo violent for our Salvation, is beyond expreffion wonderful. When I confider that all who are engaged by Duty, are either Dumb or very cold in the Matter, while you are declaiming with fo much fervour, with fo much zeal, againft the Diforders of our

our Theatres, you who have nothing to do with the matter; I can never sufficiently admire the excefs of your Zeal, which is too high and too Heavenly to be comprehended by a Mortal.

I can only fay, that 'tis a thoufand pities 'tis confin'd to fo narrow a Sphere. But, alas! good Man, it is none of your fault that it is not more univerfal. For we have reafon to be fenfible, that if you were not reftrain'd, by the apprehenfion of Brutal and Beaftly Force, you would not fail to declaim with the fame heat and the fame bitternefs againft both Church and State.

This amazing brightnefs of your Charity, has drawn upon you the Envy of fome good Men; has made you become the Hatred of Libertines, and the Jeft and Scorn of Buffoons. I Doctor am your Champion againft them all; and I have many a Bickering in your behalf, even with my moderate Friends; who are indeed for Reforming the Licentioufnefs of the Stage, but are by no means for a fuppreffion of the Play-Houfes. Mr. *Collier* fays one of them is too fevere. He does not confider the times that we live in. Thefe are not the Primitive Apoftolical Times, but the laft and Corrupt Ages of the World. The Capital of a great Kingdom muft have Meetings for publick Pleafure. If Mr. *Collier* is for pulling down Plays; let him name a more Harmlefs and Reafonable diverfion to be Eftablifhed in the room of them. What would he have us always at our Devotion? Or does he expect that we fhould be all Devout? Would he have Devotion a Mode and Fafhion, as it is in *France.* Where the Rake is as Devout as the Arch-Bifhop, the

Whore-

Whore-mafter as the Monk, and the moft inconfider-
rable Punk at *Verfaills*, as the moft Glorious Madam
de Maintenon. 'Tis true, faid he, there are things in
fome of our Plays, that I could heartily wifh were
out, but Mr. *Collier* is too rigid, too harfh, and out of
all meafure fevere. He does not bear with the leaft
faults, and feems to have no Indulgence for Human
frailty. Thus Doctor you were attack'd the other
Day by a Friend of mine, and you fhall fee how I defended you.

Lord Sir, fays I, you are the moft miftaken Man in
the World. Mr. *Collier* is no fuch Perfon as you imagine. He is a good natur'd, fweet temper'd Man as
lives. And will bear as far as any Man whatever.
And as for your faying that he has no Indulgence
for Human frailty, why 'tis a fign that you don't
know him. 'Tis true, he has taken a fatal averfion to
the Play-Houfe; and he will down with it. We have
all of us an averfion for fome thing or other. And
why fhould you be fo much concern'd for that *Rendevouz of Rakes and Strumpets ?* But yet Mr. *Collier*
has Indulgence enough for them too, any where but in
the Play-Houfe. And where's the mighty hardfhip
then upon them ? Are there no places for them to af-
femble but there? Are there not Taverns, Brandy-
Shops, Coffee-Houfes, Chocolate-Houfes, Gaming-Houfes
for the Rakes, and Indian-Houfes, Mufick-Houfes,
Bawdy-Houfes, either for Strumpets Solitary, or Strumpets and Rakes in Conjunction according as they pleafe.
Has Mr. *Collier* writ one Word for five Years together
againft any of thefe places ? For Godfake what do
you call want of Indulgence then ? Is not every Coffee-
Houfe in Town grown a Gaming-Houfe ? May not
we

we go every Hour of the Day into feveral of them,
and fee and hear twenty Fellows Swearing and Blafphe-
ming, and one furrounded by that horrid Crew.

Shaking with Bloody Oaths the Box,
And calling upon Plague and Pox.
T' affift him.

Why, there they may Swear and be damn'd for all
Mr. *Collier.* He troubles himfelf with Swearing no
where but in the Play-Houfe ? But what do you
mean by Human Frailty ? When People are wicked
in earneft that's fomething. He has nothing to fay
againft fuch. But to be Vicious in Jeft, to play the
Fool with the Devil, to counterfeit Sin forfooth on
pretence of decrying it, why thefe are *dreadful pro-*
vocations; this is flaming, and outragious wickednefs.
And wickednefs, which he is pofitively and abfolutely
refolv'd that he will not endure.

Come, Come fays he, I begin to be fenfible of the
matter. Mr. *Collier* is now declining in Years ; and
the Affairs of the World go not according to his
Wifhes. And Age and Difappointments have fowr'd
his Blood, and made him loofe the relifh of Sports and
gay Diverfions. Once more faid I, you are the moft
miftaken Man in the World ; Mr. *Collier* is far from
being a Foe to the gayeft Sports and Paftimes ; But
then he is for having thofe who frequent them take the
confent and approbation of the *Nonjuring* Clergy along
with them, who you know are *Perfons of Sobriety and*
Conduct. He'll tell you, that the Sports that good Bifhop
Laud appointed for the Sabbath, were not only fafe
but commendable. That for example, Cricket when
it

it came to be fo recommended, immediately became Canonical, Foot-Ball Orthodox, and Jugle-Cat, *Jure Divino*. But for the Layety to be fo impertinent as to chufe diverfions for themfelves; and particularly for the Ladies to believe that they have Capacities enough to Judge between right and wrong, and to diftinguifh Decency from what is not *Decorum*, he takes to be an Enormity that is never to be allow'd of in any Chriftian Country.

The Play-Houfe faid I, is one of thofe which Mr. *Collier* believes to be too Lufcious a Paftime for the Layity. To fee and to read Plays, he thinks is enough, for one of his Eftablifh'd Virtue. And it muft be own'd, that he has read or feen more than any Perfon in *Chriftendom*. As for the Layity lefs vigorous Diverfions may ferve them. The Men may take a Game at Bowls in the Summer, and a Game at Whisk in the Winter. The Women in Winter may vifit their grave Relations, and in Summer Evenings may take a Boat to cool themfelves. * For as for the *Park*, he fays, that is a place that *is too much frequented by Rakes and Strumpets. He does not mean, he fays, that all the Company there are fo; but this he may affirm he fays, that fcarce any Quarter is fometimes fo plentifully ftock'd. Now who fays Mr.* Collier, *would truft his Health in a place of Mortality, or go to the Peft-Houfe for Recreation.* Thus Mr. *Collier*, like a Perfon of Conduct and Sobriety, treats the Layity with the fame Circumfpection, that a *Romifh* Prieft does his Congregation at high Mafs, who only delivers the Wafer to the People, and referves the Wine for himfelf.

*The fame Company for the moft part that frequents the Park frequents the Play-Houfe.

But

But Doctor I had almost forgot one thing, that I urg'd among the rest in your Defence, and that was the Reason why you stick so close to the Play-House, and let some other *flaming* Vices alone, which he was pleased to enumerate. And that was that you took this way of proceeding, to be laying the Ax to the Devilish Root of the accursed Branches, that the Play-House was the undoubted Cause of all the Iniquity in the Nation; and that if we could but down with that, a suddain Reformation would follow among all sorts of People. That Porters would no longer be Drunk with Belch. That Vigorous Captains would be Tilting no more at Handsome Drawers in Taverns, that losing Gamesters would no more Blaspheme, and my Lady *Dabcheeks* Basset-Bank would be immediately broke.

These are the things that I have said in your behalf to several of the Enemies of your Short View and Defence. I now come to tell you what has happen'd upon the receiving your Disswassive; tho' 'tis scarce three-Hours since its arrival. Immediately upon the reading it, my Eldest Son *Jack* told me that he was perfectly satisfied that Plays were abominable; and taking his Hat, his Sword and his Cloak, went away for St. *James's*. My Eldest Daughter *Susan*, is gone to take a walk in the Garden, to Meditate there in the Dark; that she may have the Arguments in Readiness, by which she says she designs to Convert her Sister. But my Younger Son *Charles* made some Objections, and so did my Daughter *Harriet*, which I here send you as well as I can recollect them, because I know Doctor that you are able to answer them better than I can.

Sir,

Sir, says *Charles*, I have promis'd my Lady *Freelove* to Day, to wait upon her to the Play, and so has my Sister *Harriet*; but for the future I promise you to keep away, and so I dare say will my Sister, if you will but answer some Objections that we have to make against Mr. *Colliers* Discourses.

I know no Reason, why Mr. *Collier* should pretend to meddle with our Diversions. If he is really offended at Plays himself, in the name of God let him keep away, I know no body who is fond of his Company there. But since we don't pretend to oblige him to come, Why should he presume to oblige us to keep away?

If Mr. *Collier* is really offended at Play-Houses, I would fain know how long he has been so, or what is the Reason that he did not write against them when he was Young. For the Stage was really then more Licentious than it is now. Since he forbore writing against them till he was Old, we humbly desire that we may not leave them till we are Old. And then perhaps, we may have some natural or some politick Considerations that may oblige us to rail as much as he does.

How comes this Man to take up so much concern for us? Is it Christian Charity, and a tender care for our Souls? I would fain ask him one Question, Is not true Religion that which is chiefly necessary for the Salvation of Souls? If he says it is, Why then let me ask him another Question. Is the Religion which we of the present Establish'd Church of *England* profess the true one, or is it not? If it is, Why does not he hold Communion with us? If it is not, Why does not he set us right. Has he a concern for our

Souls

Souls or not ? . If he has, Why does he not mind the main thing ? If he has not, Why does he pretend to make us uneafie, and fet us together by the Ears about trifles ?

Is it a concern for the State that makes him take up his Pen; becaufe perhaps he believes that the Corruptions of the Stage may prove of Dangerous Confequence to the Government. But if he has that extreeam concern for it, Why does he not take an Oath to be true to it ? Why does he not Abjure the Gentleman who dwells at St. *Germains*? He believes us Schifmaticks, and he believes us Rebels, and takes no notice of the matter. But if we talk of going to a Play, the Man's Zeal grows flaming and outragious upon it. Certainly his is a very nice, and very extraordinary Charity !

But if he is offended at Plays, fo much as he pretends, Why does he fee them, why does he read them fo much ? Why fhould he be fo ridiculoufly conceited, and fo fpiritually proud, as to think that he can ftand under Temptations, under which we muft fall ?

If he has fo much averfion for Plays as he pretends, if they are fo very horrible, Why has he read fo many ? Why has he done evil that good may come of it ? If he really loves them, and they are not fo abominable, Why has he writ againft them ? If he has writ againft Plays that he loves, How comes it that he fays nothing againft the Church and State which he hates ?

D   What

What Reason can be given for that, unless that he waits for his opportunity, which by setting us at variance about trifles; he hopes in some measure to hasten, or unless, while in the Face of the World he is Bombarding the Stage, he is diligently in private undermining the Church and the State?

In this Age of universal Tolleration, when Nonsense of every Sort and Size is tollerated, not only that Gloomy, Sullen, Lifeless Nonsense, which is to be heard at *Quakers* and *Anabaptist* Meetings, but that sparkling spirited, fiery Fustian which is to be found in our Dissuasives; in an Age in which Schism it self is tollerated, Heresie is tollerated; nay, when Mr. *Collier's* Jacobite Congregation is tollerated; in this Age of universal. tolleration for Hypocrisie and Nonsense, Shall we suffer an Inquisition to be set up, for Wit, and Sense and Pleasure?

We are willing to have all the Indulgence in the World, for the Errors and Frailties of our fellow Creatures; and tho' we may believe some of them Schismaticks, believe some of them Hereticks, yet we are not for Reforming them against their Wills, nor saving them out of Malice. And we thought we might have hop'd, at least that the Government might have hop'd, that at the same time that it Indulges some of them, not only in different ways of Worship, but ways which are disagreeable, and some of them prejudicial to it, and ways which neither are, nor were, nor never will be tollerated in any other Kingdom of *Europe*; we thought, I say, that the Government might have hop'd that these very Persons would have born with a Diversion, which is Establish'd

by

Does Mr. *Collier* really believe that there is no Swearing in Gaming-Houses? No Intriegues at *India* or Chocolate-Houses? No Lying, and no Sharping in Coffee-Houses, no Beaftly Leudnefs at Mufick-Houfes, and Bawdy-Houfes? If he believes that thefe Places are Guilty of the Crimes imputed to them, Why does he not Preach to them, which have a great deal more occafion for Reformation than the Play-Houfe? For in moft of them you have Venom without Prefervative, but the Play-Houfe carries or fhould carry the Antidote with the Poifon. If Mr. *Collier* has feen any of thefe places, as 'tis hard to believe that one of his Experience fhould not have been at fome of them; methinks he fhould be convinc'd that by correcting of them, he would begin with the Head, whereas now he but pleafes and tickles Corruption, by catching Reformation by the Tail. A little common Senfe may ferve to convince a Man, that the Reforming the Stage would never Reform the Town, but the Reforming the Town would certainly Reform the Stage.

What is the Reafon then that Mr. [*Collier* neglecting the Vices of the Town, keeps fuch a Buftle at thofe of the Stage. Why becaufe it is not his defign or bufinefs to Correct or Reform any thing? His only bufinefs is to fet up himfelf. To erect an obfcure Schifmatical Parfon into a Saint of the firft Magnitude, To pafs for a Man of more Sanctity than all the Bifhops, and of more Difcernment than all the Minifters of State. His bufinefs is not to Correct and Reform, but to amufe, to puzzle, to make a Noife and a Party; to make the Stage the Apple of Diffention, to fet us at untimely Variance at this

dangerous

dangerous Juncture. He has Experience enough of
the World, to know that a Noise and a Party is
not to be made, by barely attacking of Vice. For
by doing that he would oblige only the Vertuous.
And alas they are but few; and a Silent, a Modeſt
and an Humble Party. But by attacking the Stage, he
obliges the Vitious too, and they are Numerous, and Pert,
and Arrogant, and Noiſie and Tumultuous. 'Tis
true, the Virtuous are Enemies to the Vices and
Corruptions of the Stage. But only the Guilty and
the Hypocrites are Enemies to a Stage Reform'd,
becauſe a Stage Reform'd would be Enemies only to
them. When Mr. *Collier* began to Write his ſhort
View, he deſigned to oblige only the firſt, for in the
beginning of that Book, his intent is plainly only to
Reform the Stage. But then afterwards he Wiſely
conſidered that the obliging the Virtuous would not
do his buſineſs. They are not enough to cry up their
Champion, and bring him into Reputation. But if
he appear'd an Enemy to the Stage it ſelf, and attempted to Deſtroy it inſtead of Reforming it, Why
then he would oblige all the Doubty Hectors in Virtue, a numerous multitude of falſe Branes, who would
infallibly ſtand Buff for him, and be his Bully Backs
on occaſion. He knew of old the Catalogue of
thoſe who were Enemies to Satyr, and he knew
that all the Enemies to Satyr, were ſo to the *Engliſh*
Stage.

Sunt,

Sunt, quos genus hoc minime juvat, ut pote plures
Culpari dignos, quemvis media erue Turba,
Aut ob avaritiam, aut miserâ ambitione Laboret.
Hic nuptarum infanit a moribus, hic puerorum,
Hunc capit Argenti splendor, stupet Albius ære;
Hic mutat merces surgente à sole ad eum quo
Vespertina tepet Regio, quin per mala preceps
Fertur uti pulvis collectus turbine; nequid
Summa Deperdat metuens aut ampliet ut Rem,
Omnes hi metuunt versus, odere poetas;

I know Sir, that you understand the Original very well, and there-fore I will not pretend to Interpret *Horace* to you litterally, but I desire your leave to make some Observations upon him by way of Paraphrase, which will set his Sense in a clearer light, and convince you of this Important Truth, that all who would appear what they are not, are mortal Enemies to Comedy, because the Comick Poet is perpetually upon the hunt for Originals; and every one would be glad to play the Fool or the Knave in quiet, without being sing-led from the Herd.

Sir, I shall at present trouble you, but with two of these Cha-racters of *Horace*, not only because I am sensible that I begin to tire you, but for Reasons which I shall hint to you anon, but those two Characters I desire that I may set before you with the same additi-ons, with which time has transmitted them to us, and by altering them made them Modern.

The First is he, *Qui ob avaritiam laborat.* A Gogling, Snarling, Groaning, Praying Rogue; though at the same time an Usurer and an Extortioner, a Fellow so notoriously given to cheating, that he defrauds even himsef of Necessaries, who can Dine on a Prayer as Sir *John Denham* says, and Sup on an Exhortation, one who makes a Stalking-Horse of Religion, and lyes sculking behind it with no other purpose than to draw Wild-Geese within his Reach.

The other Sir, is he; *Qui mutat merces, &c.* A Biggotted Stock-Jobber, or a Fanatick Monopolizer, a Fellow that devoutly calls

E

up

up his Family to Repetition on Sundays; and as devoutly makes them his Tools to Smuggle and Cheat the Queen on the Week-Days. A Perſon who will ſtick at no manner of Villany, but is kindly contented to be damn'd, only that his great Boobily Boy, may get half a dozen Claps, half a ſcore Surfeits, loſe half his Eſtate at the Groom-Porters, be cheated of the other half by Sharpers who are under Spur-Leathers; and Jog on to the Devil a little more gayly than his Father. In the mean time this good natur'd Father leads a moſt Exemplary Life. In the Morning while his Servants are buſie at the Water ſide, he walks about the City, to pull down Play Bills, Cheat thoſe who deal with him, to cauſe all the Beggars that he finds in his way to be Whipt; though at that very time he is going to augment the Number of them, to viſit Watch-Men, Head-Boroughs, and Petty Conſtables, and charge them that if they find any Handſome Whore upon their Watch, they ſhould bring her to him the next Morning; and leaſt the Conſtable or the Watch ſhould have a wambling to her themſelves, for ſuch things he remembers have been formerly done, he reads a long Lecture to them againſt Concupiſence, and then goes Home, and gravely Dines with his Family. The Afternoon he paſſes in walking from Tavern to Tavern, in which he Drinks above Twenty Nipperkins, in as many ſeveral Kitchens, to ſee that there is no Swearing, and no Prophaneneſs there, but that People as he thinks it behoves good Chriſtians, get Devoutly and Religiouſly Drunk; till growing more and more inflam'd with Canary and Zeal, and being full of them both, he is obliged at the laſt to Diſembogue himſelf, which he does of each, by Spewing and Preaching in turns. And after he has thus performed his Duty to the Publick; and Fortified himſelf for the better performance of private Duties, he goes home like a Good Man, to Faſt and Pray with his Family; I ſay to Faſt Sir, not out of Covetouſneſs or Superſtition, but that he may ſecure the Chaſtity of his Daughters by mortifying the Old Man in them, and the Youths of his Family.

But Sir, by your ſhaking your Head, and your biting your Lip, I am to believe you miſtake me. I am not here for making a Satyr upon the City. I know very well that this City is the only true and

ſolid

folid Foundation of the *English* Strength. Nor am I fuch a Fool as to believe that Senfe or Honour are confined to place. I am my felf acquainted with a great many Citizens, who are very Eftimable Members of the Commonwealth ; I know feveral among them who are not only Men of Senfe and Honour, but of Wit and Pleafantry. I know feveral of them, whofe true Zeal for Religion, is fhewn by all that engaging Charity, that atractive Humility, and lovely Meeknefs, which are the only figns of a good Chriftian. And for fuch true Chriftians whether they may belong to the Church or Meeting-Houfe, no Man has a greater refpect than I have ; who Judge of Mens Devotion , not by the Errors of their Underftandings, but by the Sincerity of their Hearts. But every Hypocrite, to talk in Mr. *Colliers* extraordinary Dialect, is the Difpleafure and the Difeafe of my Eyes. I Hunt him, as *Boileau* fays, as a Dog does his Game, and as foon as ever I fmell him, I bark immediately. And with fubmiffion to you Sir, I believe I am in the Right of it, and that the Hypocrites in Chriftian Warfare, ought to be more feverely handled, than a Strumpet or a Libertine, as we treat an open declar'd Enemy lefs rigoroufly than a Spy. That the number of Hypocrites in the City is very great, the Men of true Devotion there will be the firft to acknowledge. 'Tis to the Level of them that Mr. *Collier* has particularly Writ : Every thing in his fhort View, his Defence and his Diffwafive appears to be adapted to them ; the Sophiftry of his Deductions, the Equivocating and Prevaricating of his Citations, the Finicalnefs of his Language, and the Pharifaical Arrogance of his Zeal. By gaining of thefe he knew he fhould compafs both the ends, for the which he Writ. The firft of which was that he fhould engage a numerous Party to make a Noife and to Bully for him ; of which he did not fail.

For is it notorioufly known that in the late Reign, feveral Perfons of the foremention'd Stamp, who pretended to meet together for the fupport of the Laws and the Government, difcharg'd their Malice in a publick manner againft feveral Gentlemen, of known Loyalty and *English* Principles ; only that they might do an acceptable thing to a Man whom they knew to be a Mortal Enemy to the prefent Eftablifhment.

The

The other end that Mr. *Collier* probably propos'd to himself, by exasperating the Noisie and Clamorous part of the City against the Theatres, might be to Animate them against the People of Quality, whose presence supports them, and the Court whose Authority protects them. That that this is no Chimerical Conjecture, may be thought by any one who takes a short view of Mr. *Colliers* Principles. For from this proceeding he might easily forsee one of these two Consequences. For upon these Clamours and Outcries, either the Play-Houses would be supprels'd, orthey would be protected. If they were supprels'd, he easily saw the Gentry would be disoblig'd, and that would be a pretty handsome steptowards some farther Reformations, and Alterations. But if upon these Clamours they were not supprels'd, why then he had a great deal of Reason to hope that the City would grow sullen and sower. And if their being out of Humour was of such dangerous Consequence in the Days of Brother *Pryn* of blessed Memory ; when the Court appeared to have so little occasion for them, he believ'd that it might be of greater Moment now, when he knew that by the Necessity of the Times, the Court was oblig'd to Demand theirassiftance frequently.

Sir, you have often told me with extream goodness, that you requir'd no Obedience to any Commands that you laid upon us, if they did not appear to be Reasonable ; Because, God himself, you have been pleased to tell us, required only our Reasonable Service. But Sir, Can you believe it Reasonable, that I should be of another Man's Opinion against my own Sentiments, when it appears so plainly that he is not of his own ? For Sir, Can any thing be more evident than that Mr. *Collier* is moved to Write against the Stage by another Motive than that which he pretends. His Motive perhaps may be Human Policy, but it can never be Charity, or perhaps 'tis Spleen or Covetousnifs, or Pride, or Arrogance, or Fear. I say, Fear Sir. For has not Mr. *Collier* Reason to apprehend the Stage as well as Hypocrites of the foremention'd Characters? For is it not evident, that at the same time that he is setting up for a First Rate Reformer, he has shewn to the World, that he is but a Fifth-Rate Comedian ? And while he pretends to condemn Acting upon the Stage, is Acting a Part upon the Stage of the World, so awkardly

and

and fo ridicuoufly, that all who are furnifh'd with Common Senfe, have found it to be Comedy ? For whom he does he pretend to Reform? Is it not the People, as I obferv'd before, whofe Religion he abhors, and and whofe Government he hates? And does not he know very well that by Reforming our Manners, he would run Counter to his own Defigns and Wifhes; becaufe Reformation of Manners would confirm the prefent Eftablifhment, both in Church and State? and can he then really defign to Reform us? But how does he propofe to himfelf, to bring this about? Why not by fuppreffing Vice, but the Stage that Scourges and expofes it. For he meddles not with that Vice that is the World, let it be never fo *flaming and outragious.* For example, the crying Sin of *England* next to Hypocrifie, at this time is Gaming; a Sin that is attended with feveral others, both among Men and Women, as Lying, Swearing, Perjury, Fraud, Quarrels, Murders Fornication, Adultery. Has not Gaming done more mifchief in *England* within thefe laft Five Years than the Stage has done in Fifty ? For when Women have loft vaft Summs at Play, which they have been afraid to own to their Fathers or Husbands, Have they not often been known to pay them after a fhameful way ? How can the moft Inveterate Biggot pretend that Gaming is fomented or encouraged by the Stage? Muft he not on the contrary he oblig'd to own, that it is Cenfur'd and Correéted by it ? What is the Reafon then that Mr. *Collier* negleéting fo Important and fo Dangerous a Vice, againft which no body has faid one Word; referves all his Rage for the Play-Houfe ? And takes an occafion from the late Tempeft to threaten us with fome Terrible Vengeance from Heaven, if it is not immediately fuppreft. Can any thing be more ridiculous than this from him ? For does not he wifh for the greateft Vengeance that Heaven can fend down upon us? Can any Vengeance be inflicéted on a Proteftant and free People more terrible than Slavery and Idolatry ? Is not the late Tempeft, though dreadful in it felf, yet a very trifle compared to thofe? Tho' the late Storm fhould return, *and nature fhould once more appear to be in her laft Agony, and the World be Ready to expire*; would not every one, who has Noble *Englifh* Principles, chufe rather to fee it Perifh, than to lofe his Religion and his Liberty? Befides, Has the late Tempeft any thing to do with the bufinefs of the Play-Houfe? What can Mr. *Collier* mean then by threatning us with terrible Vengeance, at the fame time that he wifhes it ; and by engaging us in frivilous and groundlefs Diffentions, endeavouus all that he can to bring it on us at the very time that he pretends to avert it ?

If Mr. *Collier's* Zeal were fincere; he would neither go about to frighten us with things, which it is plain that he is not afraid of; nor neglecting more dangerous Crimes would he attack the lefs. Befides it is plain that he himfelf has not that Opinion of the Stage, into which he would Fool

and

and Delude us. For if the cause of the Stage were so bad as he would make us believe; or if it were out of Charity that he attack'd it, What need he make use of notorious falshood to decry it? 'Tis a pleasant Charity that engages a Man to be damn'd himself to Reform others. Besides, What occasion has Truth to have recourse to Falshood, which may sometimes indeed support Falshood, but must always to discerning Eyes render Truth suspected.

You know Sir, that it is easie for me to prove, that in this short Letter addrest to you Mr. *Collier*, has recourse to Falshood. For can any thing be more plain, even from the Artifice of his Address to you? Does not he here, to make the World believe, thot he has the *Countenance of Figure and Fortune*, Palm you upon the Town for a Person of Quality, who are only a private Gentleman?

If Mr. *Collier* is mov'd by Charity to exclaim thus loudly against the Stage, let me ask him one Question, Who are the Persons whom he designs to Reform? They who never come to a Play-House, methinks should have no occasion for his Corrections. If his Design is on those who come thither; Why does he not insinuate himself into their Affections, by the Meekness and Humility of his Expressions, and the Atractive Language of Charity? Why has he recourse to such Presumptuous Arrogance, as justly renders him the Aversion of some, and the Scorn of others? with him an Audience which you very well knew Sir, is often one of the most Venerable and Awful Assemblies that can be any where found, is an Assembly of Rakes and Strumpets; Buffoons are the Poets, and the Players Libertines; Does he believe that such Language is proper to work upon these People; or to provoke them and exasperate them, and render them deaf to Argument or Perswasion.

Besides there is something in Mr. *Colliers* Style with which Truth is almost incompatible, and that is Affectation, which is always false. Truth is plain and simple, and natural, and as she can have no defect in her is but hid by Ornament. 'Tis true when we convey her to the Understanding by the Passions, we sometimes give her Ornament. But then that Ornament must be in nature and consequently true. But Affectations always false and can no more consist with truth than darkness can with light. What I have observed of Man in general, my be said of Writers; That Affectation is a certain sign in them of want of Sincerity, or of Understanding, and very often of both.

But Mr *Collier's* is the most affected, most Foppish Style that ever I met with in Ancient or Modern Authors; of which I will undertake to convince any Impartial Man, if he is but a tolerable judge of writing.

But to return from Words to Things, I have not time enough to display the perpetual Sophistry of his Inferences, or rather his no Inferences,

for

for a Metaphor or an Allegory is with him an Argument, and so is often an Hyperbole. But I shall say a word of the more than Jesuitical prevaricating in his Authorities I shall only insist upon too, the one of which he brings from Old, and the other from Modern *Rome*.

Pray Sir, Let me see Mr. *Collier's* Letter ; Ay, here the Authorities are.

The Republick of Rome, *before* Julius Cæsar *stopt the building of a Theatre, being fully convinc'd, that this diversion would bring in Foreign Vice, that the old* Roman *Virtue would be lost, and the Spirits of the People Emasculated.*

To prove this he refers his Reader to his Defence of the Short View. That is, he endeavours to support the Sham which he puts upon the World now, by that which he put upon it five Years ago. 'Tis true after all, Mr. *Collier* speaks the Truth here, but 'tis dash'd and brew'd with a Vengeance. 'Tis true, the *Romans* did stop the building of a Theatre, before the Time of *Cæsar*. But would he pass this upon us for one Act of the *Roman* People, or for their constant Sense ? If for their constant Sense, their constant practise proves that it was quite contrary. If for one Act, of what validity can that possibly be against their constant Sense ?

Is not Mr. *Collier* now a most shameful Hyocrite ? For does not he know that the *Romans* had the highest veneration for Plays imaginable ? Is not every School-Boy, who has read *Terence* convinc'd of it ? Do not his Comedies tell us by their Titles that they were part of the Religion of that People ? That they were all acted at their Funeral Ceremonies, or at the Festivals of their Gods?

That which he has said of Q *Elizabeth* is another Pious Fraud, a meer Religious Banter. But I know that you who are so well acquainted with the History of our Nation must be already satisfied of it.

But the Pope has lately shut up the Theatres in *Italy* ? Can any thing be more absurd than this ? Has the Pope lately shut up the Bawdy-Houses ? Or does he continue to lay a Tax upon Sin, and to give them Spiritual Licenses ? 'Tis very certain he does. What then would Mr. *Collier* conclude from this; that the Government here ought to License Bawdy-Houses, and to Suppress Play-Houses, because the Pope takes the same Method ?

I think Sir, I have made it plainly appear, that Mr. *Collier* is one who has Reason to be afraid of Theatres, and therefore to hate them. For he is one of those with a Vengance who endeavour to appear what they are not. And tho' now a Days a Priest is not suffer'd to be brought upon the Stage, yet I question whether he is to be regarded as a Priest, who wears a Sword of five Foot long, and a Perruke of three, and goes about Reforming in the same Habit, in which the *French* Dragoons are at this very Juncture Piously Reforming the *Cevennois*.

Thus Sir, I desire that I may have leave to continue to be a Friend to our Theatres, since I have clearly shewn that Mr. *Collier* is not from his

Heart

Heart their Enemy; especially since I am convinc'd that the Play-Houses with all their Immorality and with all their faults, may be instrumental to the Reforming so Profligate an Age as this.

Thus Doctor, I have sent the summ of the Objections which were made by *Charles*, to which I desire your Answer, that the Boy who is Hot, and Opinionated, may not run on in his Error.

As soon as he had done, I took *Harriet* to task, Daughter said I, You see the Case is very hard upon you and the rest of your Sex, for thus the Doctor puts it, *Either the Ladies are pleas'd with the Indecencies of the Stage or they are not. If they are pleas'd, 'tis a hard Imputation on their Virtue. If they are not pleased, 'twill be enquired why they come there.* For his part, *He confesses that he has not Logick enough to disengage you.*

While I spoke this, I perceived some great alteration in her; you would have sworn, *her Imagination had been shock'd, her Aversion put into a fit, and that she underwent much Fatigue of Fancy and Mortification.* To speak more vulgarly, the Blood began to spring up into her Face, her little Breasts began to heave, and she darted a frown that made her awful ev'n to me her Father. He wants Logick to disengage us, (said she, with a disdainful Air, after I had just repeated those very Words,) why, then he shall find that I have more than he has, and that I who have not yet reach'd my Seventeenth Year, am able to make a very just Apology in behalf of my self, and all the Women of Condition in *England*, whom he has so basely affronted. Tho' we are not pleas'd with the Indecencies or Immoralities of Plays, yet notwithstanding that we frequent them, because some Diversion is absolutely necessary for us, and because perhaps ev'n Modern Plays with all the faults imputed to them, are the most Innocent of the Diversions which this Town affords.

The Diversions that the Town affords, are chiefly reduc'd to four, 1, Gaming. 2. Musick-Meetings. 3. Balls and Meetings for Dancing. 4. Going to Plays. Now of all these, I am apt to believe that Plays are the most Innocent, for the following Reasons. They raise the Passions only to correct them, whereas the others raise 'em merely for the sake of inflaming 'em. The Plays, and more especially Tragedies instruct us in Virtue, which the other Diversions do not. They improve us in Lawful Innocent Knowledge, which in some measure supplies the want of Education in our Sex. They form our Language, and polish our Minds, and so Capacitate us, when we come to Marry, to engage and endear our Husbands to us. For we every Day see that only Fools are constant long to Fools. Sir, in short the Case is thus. Diversions the Ladies of a great Metropolis must have. I have particulariz'd the several Diversions which this Town affords. All the Danger, and all the Temptation which this Judicious Persons supposes to be at the Play-House, are really in all the other Diversions, which have none of the advantages that may be reap'd from Tragedies, for the Improvemǎnt either of our Virtue or Knowledge. Why then would this mighty Reformer have us leave Plays for them ? Would he have us have no Diverſion, or would he have us make choice of thoſe which have the moſt Temptation ?

True Sir, there are paſſages in ſome of our Plays which I could heartily wiſh were out. But does he think the Virtue of the Ladies who frequent Play-Houſes, is ſo very weak, as to be o'erthrown by the Luſciouſneſs, as he calls it, of a Scriblers *Double Entendres*. What have ſo many great Examples as we find on the Stage, ſo many Noble and Generous Sentiments, ſo many accompliſh'd patterns of Virtue ; Have all theſe no manner of pow'r to rouze, to ſtrengthen and inflame our Virtue ; and ſhall two or three wretched Equivocalls, three or four miſerable *Double Entendres* have the force to corrupt us ?

If any of my Sex happen to find themſelves ſo infirm, as this worthy Reformer appears to own that he is ; if two or three ridiculous double-meanings have ſtrength enough to undo them, in ſpight of thoſe exalted Heroick Characters, which in my Opinion ſhould be enough to fix our Affections on Virtue to that degree, that nothing that we meet with abroad in the World ſhould have the pow'r to move us ; if any of my Sex are ſo infirm, let them in God's name keep away from our Theatres. But I find no ſuch ſcandalous weakneſs about me. I can deſpiſe a Fool who thinks to entertain me with his ſordid playing on Words, but at the ſame time can be entertain'd with Wit and good Senſe, and more with the Innocence of true writ Humour, and I can be both pleas'd and mov'd, with the excellent Scenes of an Inſtructive Tragedy : Does this Judicious Perſon really believe that the Converſations which we find in the World are Virtue and Purity all. The Food of the Mind like that of the Body is not all of it fit for Nouriſhment. But ſtrong Virtue like ſtrong Nature knows how to diſcern and ſeparate, to reject the bad, to aſſimilate the good by which it is fed and ſupported. If any of my Sex have the ſcandalous weakneſs to have their Virtue and their Honour endanger'd by the Folly of *Double Enten-dres*, I would adviſe them to take their leaves of the Play-Houſe. But at the ſame time I would adviſe Mr. *Collier* to perſwade his Noble Patrons of the Reforming Club, to erect a Proteſtant Nunnery for them, for nothing leſs can ſecure them. For they who are found ſo ſtrangely weak as to be warm'd by a meer Painted Fire , How can they ever ſtand againſt the real Flames of Love ?

How many extraordinary Women may *England* boaſt of, ſince Plays were introduc'd among us ? Among whom are three of the greateſt Queers that ever the World produc'd ; and all of them took Delight in Plays: How

many

many Ladies of Inferiour Rank have frequented, and still frequent 'em, who yet in proportion are fam'd for every Virtue. What does this Charitable Person believe of our Mothers, our Aunts and Grandmothers? Does he believe them Adultresses all because they frequented the Play-House? But you Sir have Justice to believe better. You knew my Mother true to your Bed, as she was dear to your Arms. And I beseech you to have the goodness to believe, that tho' like her I frequent our Theatres I will be always Heir to her Virtue, as I am to her likeness.

This Doctor was the sum of what *Harriet* said before she went to the Play. News is just now brought me that she is come back from that horrid place, and is gone with *Charles* to my Lady *Freeloves*, and that her Ladyship has sent for me——

Ah dear Doctor, Let me see you to morrow, to receive some Consolation from you. For here have happen'd two of the most unfortunate things in the World. For News is brought me from *Piccadilly* that *Jack* has lost a Thousand Pound at Picket, and *Susan* who went into the Garden forsooth to Meditate, tho' she went out as black as a Raven, being in Mourning for her Great Aunt, yet as I hope for Mercy the Jade is return'd as white and as powder'd, as if she had been hard at work in a Bolting-House. So that I could wish that for this one Night, they had both been with *Harriet* and with *Charles* at the Tabernacle of the Wicked.

I am, Dear Doctor, Yours, &c.

POSTSCRIPT.

SINCE I writ this, I have seen a Letter written by you, tho' without Name to Mrs--- She designs to return you an Answer, as soon as some little Affairs will give her leave. In the mean while she says, that in the hurry in which your Letter seems to be Writ, you overlook'd the First part of the Passage which you quoted from Doctor *Tillotson*, and therefore she desir'd me to Transcribe it, and to send it you with this, which in Obedience to her Commands I have done, and it is as follows, *Tillot. Serm. vol. 1. To speak against them* (viz. Plays) *in general, may be thought too Severe, and that which the present Age cannot so well brook, and would not perhaps be so just and reasonable, because it is very possible they might be so fram'd, and governed by such rules, as not only to be innocently diverting, but instructing and useful ; to put some Vices and Follies out of Countenance, which cannot perhaps be so decently reprov'd, nor so effectually expos'd and corrected any other way.* p. 320

FINIS.

Page 1. in the Date, for *Jan.* 27th. read *Jan.* the 12.

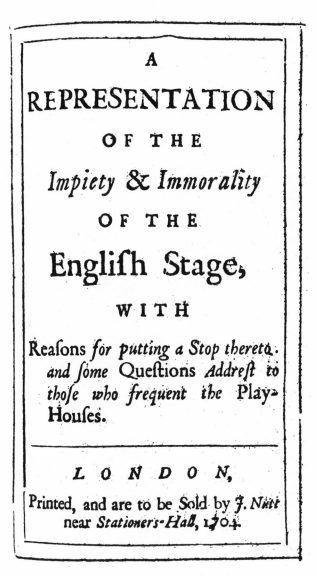

A

REPRESENTATION

OF THE

Impiety & Immorality

OF THE

English Stage,

WITH

Reasons *for putting a Stop thereto.*
and some Questions *Addrest to*
those who frequent the Play-
Houses.

L O N D O N,

Printed, and are to be Sold by *J. Nutt*
near *Stationers-Hall,* 1704.

A REPRESENTATION
OF THE
Impiety & Immorality
OF THE
Englifh Stage.

THE various Methods that have been ufed for Preventing the outragious and infufferable Diforders of the STAGE, having been in a great meafure defeated: It is thought proper, under our prefent Calamity, and before the approaching FAST, to collect fome of the *Prophane and Immoral Expreffions* out of feveral late PLAYS, and to put them together in a little Compafs, that the Nation may thereby be more convinced of the *Impiety of the Stage*, the Guilt of fuch as frequent it, and the Neceffity of putting a Stop thereto, either

by

by a total Suppreſſion of the *Play-Houſes*,
as was done in the Reign of Queen *Elizabeth*, or by a Suſpenſion for ſome conſiderable time, after the Example of other Na-
tions; where, we are informed, the Stages
were very chaſte, in reſpect of ours of this
Nation, who are of a Reformed Religion,
and do with ſo much Reaſon glory in
being of the beſt conſtituted Church in
the World; nay, 'tis out of doubt but the
Theatres even of *Greece* and *Rome* under
Heatheniſm, were leſs obnoxious and offen-
ſive, which yet by the Primitive Fathers
and General Councils ſtood condemned.

And is not the dangerous and expenſive
War we are engaged in, together with
the preſent Poſture of Affairs, a ſufficient
Reaſon for this, tho' the Play-Houſes were
leſs miſchievous to the Nation than they
are?

Are we not alſo loudly called upon to
lay aſide this prophane Diverſion, by the
late dreadful Storm, terrible beyond that
which we are told was felt in the Year
1636? which, as a Right Reverend Prelate
has obſerv'd, ſome good Men then thought
preſag'd further Calamity to this Nation,
and was accordingly followed by the Com-
motions

(5)

motions in *Scotland* the very next Year, and not long after by the Civil War in *England*.

And if we go on to countenance such open and flagrant Defiances of Almighty God, have we not great Reason to fear his heavy Judgments will consume us?

But further, Her Majesty having now, upon Occasion of the late great Calamity, appointed a Day of Solemn Fasting and Humiliation throughout the Kingdom, for the deprecating of God's Wrath, surely the Players have little Reason to expect that they shall still go on in their abominable Outrages; who, 'tis to be observed with Indignation, did, as we are assured, within a few Days after we felt the late dreadful Storm, entertain their Audience with the ridiculous Representation of what had fill'd us with so great Horror in their Plays call'd *Mackbeth* and the *Tempest*, as if they design'd to Mock the Almighty Power of God, *who alone commands the Winds and the Seas, and they obey him.* No surely, it cannot but be hoped, that a Suspension at least of the Players acting for some considerable time will follow, when the *Prophaneness and Immorality of the Stage comes* to Her Majesty's Knowledge, who, 'tis to

A 3

be remembred, has never once given any
Countenance to the Play-Houfe by Her
Royal Prefence, fince Her happy Acceffion
to the Throne.

The abominable obfcene Expreffions
which fo frequently occur in our Plays,
as if the principal Defign of them was to
gratifie the lewd and vicious part of the
Audience, and to corrupt the virtuoufly
difpos'd, are in this black Collection wholly
omitted; left thereby frefh Poifon fhould
be adminiftred inftead of an Antidote.

After the Endeavours ufed by Sir
Richard Blackmore, Mr. Collier,
and others, to Correct and Reform
the Scandalous Diforders *and*
Abufes *of the* Stage *were found*
tob unfuccefsful; in the Year 1699,
feveral of the Players *were profecu-*
ted in the Court of Common-Pleas,
upon the Statute of 3 Jac. 1. *for*
prophanely ufing the Name of GOD
upon the Stage, *and Verdicts were*
obtained againft them.

And

And in Easter-Term, 1701, *the*
Players *of one* House *were Indicted*
at the King's - Bench - Bar, *before*
the Right Honourable *the* Lord
Chief Justice Holt, *for using these*
following Expressions, and were there-
of Convicted.

In the Play call'd, The Provok'd Wife.

'But more than all that, you must know
'I was afraid of being damn'd in those
'Days; for I kept sneaking, cowardly
'Company, Fellows that went to Church,
'and said Grace to their Meat, and had
'not the least Tincture of Quality about
'em.

'Damn'em both, with all my Heart; and
'every thing else that daggles a Petticoat;
'except four generous Whores, with *Betty*
'*Sands* at the Head of 'em, who were
'drunk with my Lord *Rake* and I, ten
'times in a Fortnight.

'Sure, if Woman had been ready crea-
'ted, the Devil, instead of being kick'd
'down into Hell, had been married.

A 4   'Pox

'Pox of my Family.
'Pox of her Virtue.
'He has married me, and be damn'd to
'him.
'* Pox of the Parfon.
'Damn Morality, and damn the Watch.
'Let me fpeak and be damn'd:
'And you and your Wife may be damn'd.
'Stand off and be damn'd.
'Damn me, if you han't.
'Lord! What Notions have we filly
'Women from thefe old Philofophers of
'Virtue, for Virtue is this, and Virtue is
'that, and Virtue has its own Reward;
'Virtue, Virtue is an Afs, and a Gallant is
'worth forty on't.
'If I fhould play the Wife and Cuckold
'him.
'That would be playing the down-right
'Wife indeed.
'I know according to the ftrict Statute
'Law of Religion, I fhou'd do wrong; but
'if there were a Court of *Chancery* in Hea-
'ven, I'm fure I fhou'd caft him.
'If there were a Houfe of Lords you
'might.
'If you fhould fee your Miftrefs at a
'Coronation, dragging her Peacocks

* *This is fpoken by one in a Minifter's Habit.*

'Train,

' Train, with all her State and Infolence
' about her, it would ftrike you with all
' the awful Thoughts that Heaven it felf
' could pretend to, from you.

' Madam, to oblige your Ladyfhip, he
' fhall fpeak Blafphemy.

' In hopes thou'lt give me up thy Body,
' I refign thee up my Soul.

' A Villain, but a repenting Villain;
' Stuff which Saints in all Ages have been
' made of.

' Satan and his Equipage; Woman,
' tempted me, Luft weaken'd me, and fo,
' the Devil overcame me; as fell *Adam*,
' fo fell I.

A Bill was likewife found againft the
Players of the other Houfe, in the
Term abovementioned, for the fol-
lowing Expreffions; but the Indict-
ment being wrong laid, they were
acquitted: but they were Indicted
the Term following for the fame,
which Indictment is not yet tried.

In the Humour of the Age.

' Marriage, that was only contriv'd for
' the

‘ the meaner Rank ; tell me of Marriage,
‘ commend me to a Whore.
  ‘ Every ferious Thought, was fo much
‘ Time loft.
  ‘ We addrefs you with the fame awful
‘ Reverence we petition Heaven.

In Sir Courtly Nice.

  ‘ Nay, his Salvation is a Looking-Glafs,
‘ for there he finds his eternal Happinefs,
‘ Surly’s Heaven, at leaft his Prieft is his
‘ Claret-Glafs, for to that he confeffes all
‘ his Sins, and from it receives Abfolution
‘ and Comfort. But his Damnation is a
‘ Looking-Glafs, for there he finds an e-
‘ ternal Fire in his Nofe.
  ‘ That fame thing, the Word *Love*, is a
‘ Fig-Leaf to cover the naked Senfe, a
‘ Fafhion brought up by *Eve*, the Mother
‘ of Jilts, fhe Cuckold her Hufband with
‘ the Serpent, then pretended to Modefty,
‘ and fell a making of Plackets.
  ‘ Let him be in Mifery and be damn’d.
  ‘ And a Pox on thee for’t.
  ‘ Prithee Drefs and be damn’d.
  ‘ Pox on ’em : Pox on you all Whores.
  ‘ Pox take him.
  ‘ Rot me.
  ‘ Let him Plague you, Pox you, and
‘ damn you; I don’t care and be damn’d.
                                    The

*The following Expreſſions are tranſ-
cribed out of the Plays that have been
Acted and Printed ſince they were
Indicted for the horrid Paſſages
above-recited.*

In the Comedy call'd,

The Falſe Friend. 1702.

Pag. 7. ' Pox take ye. *Pag. 12* ' The
' Devil fetch me, &c.

Pag. 22. ' Heaven's Bleſſing muſt needs
' fall upon ſo dutiful a Son; but I don't
' know how its Judgments may deal with
' ſo indifferent a Lover.

Pag. 28. ' Say that 'tis true, you are
' married to another, and that a ——
' 'Twou'd be a Sin to think of any Body
' but your Husband, and that —— You
' are of a timorous Nature, and afraid of
' being damn'd.

' How have I lov'd, to Heaven I appeal;
' but Heaven does now permit that Love
' no more.

' Why does it then permit us Life and
' Thought? Are we deceiv'd in its Omni-
' potence? Is it reduc'd to find its Plea-
' ſure in its Creature's Pain?

Pag. 33.

Pag. 33. *Leonora's* Charms turn Vice
' to Virtue, Treason into Truth ; Nature,
' who has made her the Supream Object
' of our Desires must needs have design'd
' her the Regulator of our Morals.

'There he goes I'faith ; he seem'd as if
' he had a Qualm just now ; but he never
' goes without a Dram of Conscience-water
' about him to set Matters right again.

Pag. 43. 'Speak, or by all the Flame
' and Fire of Hell eternal ; speak, or thou
' art dead.

In the Inconftant, *or the* Way to Win him. 1702.

Pag. 10. ' My Blessing ! Damn ye, you
' young Rogue.

Pag. 20. What do you pray for ? Why,
' for a Husband ; that is, you implore Pro-
' vidence to assist you in the just and pious
' Design of making the wisest of his Crea-
' tures a Fool, and the Head of the Crea-
' tion a Slave.

Pag. 43. ' But don't you think there is
' a great deal of Merit in dedicating a beauti-
' ful Face to the Service of Religion ?

' Not half so much as devoting them
' to a pretty Fellow. If our Femality had
' no

' no Bufinefs in this World, why was it fent
' hither? Let's dedicate our beautiful Minds
' to the Service of Heaven: And for our
' handfom Perfons, they become a Box at
' the Play, as well as a Pew in the Church.

In the Modifh Husband.

Pag. 12. ' She's mad with the Whimfies
' of Virtue and the Devil.

Pag. 28. ' I think Wit the moft imper-
' tinent thing that belongs to a Woman,
' except Virtue.

Pag. 47. ' The Devil fetch him.

Pag. 50. ' I'm going towards Heaven,
' Sirrah; it muft be the Way to my Mi-
' ftrefs.

In the Play call'd, Vice Reclaim'd, &c.

Pag. 15. ' Now the Devil take that
' dear falfe agreeable; what fhall I call him,
' *Wilding.* But I'll go home and pray
' heartily we may meet again to morrow.
' By Heaven, &c.

Pag. 24. ' By Heaven it becomes you.

Pag. 27. ' The Devil take me.

Pag. 31. ' Lightning blaft him! Thun-
' der rivet him to the Earth! That Vulture,
' Confcience, prey upon his Heart, and
' rack him to Defpair!   *Pag.* 32.

Pag. 32. Grant me, ye Powers, one
' lucky Hint for Mischief.

 Pag. 43. ' Then damn me, if I don't, &c.

 Pag. 47. ' Rot me and be damn'd.

 Pag 52. ' By Heaven, &c.

 Pag. 60. ' Well, the Devil take me.

In *the* Different Widows.

 Pag. 1. ' Damn'd Lies, by *Jupiter* and
' *Juno*, and the rest of the Heathen Gods
' and Goddesses; for I remember I paid
' two Guinea's for swearing Christian
' Oaths last Night.

 Pag. 2. Pox take him. *Pag.* 24. Ye im-
' mortal Gods, who the Devil am I?

 Pag. 61. ' May the Devil, Curses,
' Plagues and Disappointments light upon
' you.

In *the* Fickle Shepherdess.

 Pag. 17. Bid *Charon* instantly prepare
' his Boat, I'd row to Hell.

 Ibid. O *Ceres*, can thy all-seeing
' Eye *behold* this Object, and yet restrain
' thy Pity?

Pag. 32.

Pag. 32. 'Fly hence to Hell; there hide
'thy Head lower than Darkneſs. Wou'd
'thou hadſt been acting Inceſt, Murder,
'Witchcraft, when thou cam'ſt to pray :
'Thou hadſt in any thing ſinn'd leſs than
'in this Devotion.

Pag. 36. 'Where Love's blind, **God**
'ſends forth continual Arrows.

Pag. 42. '*Ceres,* to whom we all things
'owe.

Pag. 46. '**Almighty** *Ceres.*

In the Play called,

Marry or do Worſe, 1704.

Pag. 4. 'Pox on me. Rot the World.
Pag. 6. Pox on him.
Pag. 8. ' A Plague on her.
'The Devil take you for a Witch.
'The Devil take you for a Fool.
Pag. 12. 'No Matrimony; the Devil
'danced at the firſt Wedding there was,
'and Cuckoldom has been in Faſhion ever
'ſince.
'The Devil take you for me.
Pag. 12, & 13. 'The Devil's in't if he
'been't fit for Heaven, when my Maſter
'has writ Cuckoldom there.

The

The Devil take me, &c.

Pag. 18. A Plague choak you.

Pag. 21. A smart Jade by Heaven.

Pag. 33. Now the Devil take him, &c.

Pag. 37. ' A Plague on my Master.

Pag. 44. The Devil take me, &c.

Pag. 47. ' I pity him, and yet a Pox ' on him too.

Pag. 51. ' That dear damn'd Virtue of ' hers tempts me strangely.

Pag. 54. ' The Devil take me, &c.

Pag. 64. ' By Heaven.

It must be again remembred, that the detestable lewd Expressions contained in the abovementioned Plays, which seem to be the most pernicious part of our Comedies, are not here recited, least they should debauch the Minds and corrupt the Manners of the Reader, and do the same Mischief, in some degree, as they do in the greatest when used upon the Stage, tho' mentioned with never so great Indignation. And it must be likewise taken notice of, that these Instances of the prophane Language of Plays, which the good Christian will read with Horror, would not have been put together, and laid before the World, had not the Incorrigibleness of the Players made it necessary for the Ends abovementioned.

And now may not these plain Questions be proposed, without Offence, to the Persons who frequent our Play-Houses ; and especially to such of them as appear at any times in our Churches, and at the Holy Sacrament, and be submitted to the Judgment of all Mankind.

I. Can Persons who frequent the *Play-Houses*, and are not displeased to hear Almighty God blasphemed, his Providence questioned and denied, his Name prophaned, his Attributes ascribed to sinful Creatures, and even to Heathen Gods, his Holy Word burlesqued, and treated as a Fable, his Grace made a Jest of, his Ministers despised, Conscience laught at, and Religion ridiculed ; in short, the Christian Faith and Doctrine exposed, and the sincere Practice of Religion represented as the Effect of Vapours and Melancholy, Virtue discountenanced, and Vice encouraged, Evil treated as Good, and Good as Evil, and all this highly aggravated by being done in cool Blood, upon Choice and Deliberation ? Can those, I say, that

B   frequent

frequent the *Play-Houses*, and are not difpleafed with any of thefe things, be thought to have any due Senfe of Religion?

II. Can Perfons who often fpend their Time and Money to fee Plays, be fuppos'd to be difpleas'd with, and to have a due Indignation at, the Hearing the Outrages beforementioned, which fo often occur in them, and of which there is a difmal Specimen laid before the World in this Paper?

III. Can fincere Chriftians encourage and affift, by their Prefence and Purfes, Men in committing fuch Practices, if they ferioufly reflect on the fatal Confequences of them?

IV. Can any who have a true Concern for the Honour of Almighty God, give Countenance and Support to fuch Entertainments whereby he is fo difhonour'd and affronted, though they could fuppofe themfelves above the Danger of being the worfe for them, which they can never be?

V. Can Perfons who know 'tis generally allowed, that the Infidelity and
Loofe-

Loofenefs of the Age is very much owing
to the Play-Houfes; who have obferved,
that the Zeal of particular Perfons have
decreafed, and their Strictnefs of Life a-
bated, by their going to Plays; and do
think that the Gofpel obliges them to
difcourage, by their Reproof and Example,
Sin in their Neighbours, to endeavour,
according to their Advantages and Opportunities, to further their fpiritual Welfare, and to be *Lights* to lead others in their
Duty and Way to Heaven? Can fuch, tho'
they could think themfelves wholly fecure
from taking Infection in going to the Play-
Houfe, encourage others, even weak and
feeble Chriftians, by their Example, to run
to the fame dangerous Place likewife? Can
this be thought an Expreffion of their Charity to their Neighbour, or to be acceptable to Almighty God? or rather, Should
not Compaffion to the Souls of their
Neighbours keep fuch as have a due Concern for them from going to fuch Places?

VI. Can it be denied, but that the
going of a few fober Perfons, tho' but
once a Year, to fee a Play, that they
think lefs offenfive and dangerous, does
encourage many others to go frequently
to Plays, and to thofe that are more abo-

B 2   minably

minably loose and prophane; who might never go at all to them, if none frequented them but such as were entirely abandoned to Shame as well as Vice?

VII. Can Persons who have good Dispositions to Religion, who go but once or twice in a Year to the *Play-House*, say, upon their Experience, that they think the seeing of Plays is proper to encrease the Love of God in Men, to fit them for holy Exercises, and to promote their spiritual Welfare? or rather, Must they not own, that by the seeing of Plays they are more indisposed for Religious Performances; that the Awe and Reverence which they had for God and Religion, and the Horrour which they had at the Sins which they there see Men divert themselves with, and make a Jest of, does thereby wear off; that their sensual Desires are more heightned and enflamed; that they are more alienated from God, and more enamoured with the World?

VIII. Can Persons who are sensible of, and do heartily lament their want of the Love and Fear of God, their too great a Love of the World, the frequent Distractions of their Mind in Prayer, and the Unruliness of their Lusts and Passions, delight to frequent
a Place

a Place where they are furrounded with
Temptations to the Love of the World;
where what can excite to unlawful Defires
and Actions is promoted; and the Arts of
an eafie Defilement are ftudied? Can they
think this confiftent with the Rules of
keeping from all Appearance of Evil, of
avoiding the Occafions and Temptations
to Sin, and that Watchfulnefs over their
Thoughts, and that Diligence in making
their Calling and Election fure, as the Gofpel requires? Do they in any wife herein
adorn their Profeffion, refemble the Chriftians who lived in the firft Ages of Chriftianity; or thofe who in any Age fince
have been celebrated for their Virtue?

IX. Can Perfons in good earneft pray,
as they are directed in the Lord's-Prayer,
Not to be led into Temptation, and yet frequent the Play-Houfe, where they are af-
faulted with more and greater Temptations than incounter them perhaps in any
other Place?

X. Can fuch Perfons as go to the *Play-
Houfes* on Week-days, and appear in our
Churches on the Lord's-day, and even at
the Holy Sacrament, where they declare,
that they *prefent themfelves, their Souls and*
Bodies,

*Bodies, as a reasonable, holy and lively Sa-
crifice to God,* be suppos'd to attend upon
these Holy Ordinances with a suitable
Frame of Mind; since the Language and
Design of Sermons, and of our Liturgy,
and of Plays, are so different and even directly contrary to each other?

XI. Can Ladies really dislike Lewd Dif-
course in Conversation, and yet like to see
Lewdness represented in all the Dresses that
can vitiate the Imagination, and fasten upon the Memory?

XII. Can Parents, or any other Persons
who have the Conduct of Youth, and
have any serious Concern for the Souls of
their Children, or of those that are committed to their Care, satisfie their Consciences, without Restraining them from
going to a place of such Impiety and Infection; where they would be in the
way to unlearn the best Instructions of
their Parents and Governours; where
Pride and Falshood, Malice and Revenge,
Injustice and Immodesty, Contempt of
Marriage, and false Notions of Honour,
are recommended; where Men are taught
to call in question the first Principles of
their Religion, and are led to a contempt
of Sacred things?   XIII

XIII. Can fincere and judicious Chrifti-ans think that the Players expofing (as they pretend to do) Formality, Humour, and Pedantry, is an Equivalent for their infulting facred things, and their promo-ting to fo high a degree the Prophanenefs and Debauchery of the Nation?

XIV. Can modeft and prudent Chri-ftians think, that the Opinion of the Ge-neral Councils, Primitive Fathers, and fo many wife and good Men in the feveral Ages of the Church, who have con-demned the going to Plays as unlawful, and as a renouncing the Baptifmal Engage-ments, doth not deferve great regard?

XV. Can fincerely religious Perfons hear of this moft horrid, licentious Treat-ment of facred things as is in our Plays, and this not among *Mahometans* and *In-fidels*, not at *Rome* and *Venice*, but in a Proteftant Countrey, and upon the *En-glifh* Stage, without a Fear that the Judg-ments of God will fall upon us?

XVI. Can lefs be expected from good Chriftians, who are fenfible of the into-lerable Diforders of the Play-Houfes, and
the

the Mifchiefs that are brought upon Mankind by them, than that they would ufe
all proper Methods for the Difcouraging
and Reftraining their Relations and Friends
from going to them, as they have any
Concern for the Honour of God, the Good
of Mankind, and the Welfare of their own
Immortal Souls?

XVII. Laftly, Can Perfons frequent
the Play-Houfes, after the outragious Im-
pieties of them, and the fatal Effects of
their going to them, are in fo full and ad-
vantageous a manner laid open to the
World, without a greater Aggravation of
their Guilt?

F I N I S.

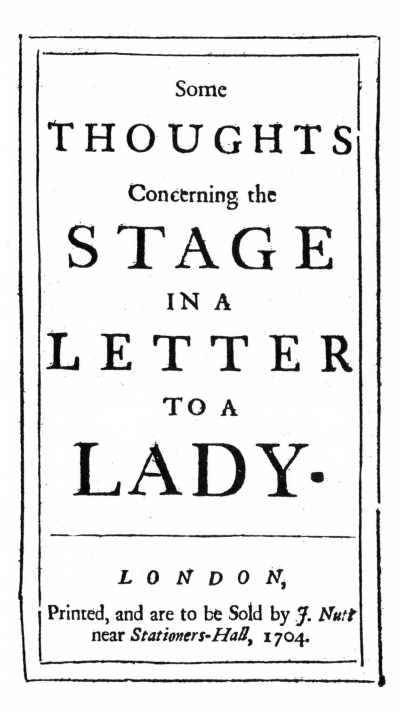

Some

THOUGHTS

Concerning the

STAGE

IN A

LETTER

TO A

LADY.

LONDON,

Printed, and are to be Sold by *J. Nutt*
near *Stationers-Hall*, 1704.

Madam,

IT is with no little Pleasure I behold you treading in the Paths of *Virtue*, and practifing the Duties of a Holy and Religious Life. This, as it has deſervedly gain'd you the Love and Admiration of all that know you : ſo, I doubt not, but you will always find it a *Fund* of ſolid Peace and Satisfaction to your own Mind. I heartily wiſh there were many more ſuch bright Examples in the World, that the Ladies might be at laſt convinc'd, *That there is ſomething worthy their Imitation beyond the Modes of Dreſs and Equipage ; ſomething which will render them much more agreeable to the beſt and wiſeſt of their Admirers, and, in time, no leſs pleaſing to themſelves.* I make no doubt but the Age (as corrupt as it is) can furniſh us with many Inſtances of thoſe of your *Sex*, who think the Beauty of the Mind does far ſurpaſs the gay Appearances of the moſt ſplendid Outſide. But yet, it muſt be confeſſed, that there

are

are others, (and those not a few) whose
Lives are almoft one continued Circle of
Vanity and Folly. Such as divide the beft
and moft precious part of their Time between their *Toilet*, the *Exchange*, and the
Play-Houfe. This, I believe, upon Enquiry,
will appear to be no unjuft Cenfure ; tho'
at the fame time, *Madam*, I muft freely
own to you, that I think it a moft a-
mazing thing, that the *Ladies* (at leaft
thofe who make any Pretenfions to Virtue and Goodnefs) fhould ever be feen at
the laft of thefe Places, where they find
themfelves fo fcandaloufly treated. I am
apt to think, that very few of 'em have
read Mr. *Collier's View of the Stage* ; if
they had, they would there fee the *Corruptions* of the Plays fet in fo clear a Light,
that one would believe, they fhould never after be Tempted to appear in a Place
where *Lewdnefs* and *Obfcenity* (not to
mention other Immoralities) are fo great
a part of the Entertainment ; a Place that
is now become the *Common Rendezvouz* of
the moft Lewd and Diffolute Perfons ;
the *Exchange*, (if I may fo call it) where
they meet to carry on the *vileft* and *worft*
of Practices. 'Tis the Nurfery of all manner of *Wickednefs*, where the Seeds of
Atheifm

Atheism and *Irreligion* are sown, which
Weak and Tender Minds too readily cul-
tivate, and from thence are easily led into
a *Contempt* of all that's Serious.   It is impossible to say, how many, and how great
the *Mischiefs* are that spring from thence;
which if a Man should take a View of, it
would, perhaps, be one of the most Melancholy Prospects that ever he beheld.   To
look into our *Modern Plays*, and there to see
the Differences of Good and Evil confounded, Prophaneness, Irreligion, and
Unlawful Love, made the masterly Stroaks
of the *fine Gentleman* ; Swearing, Cursing, and Blaspheming, the Graces of his
Conversation; and Unchristian Revenge,
to consummate the Character of the *Hero*;
Sharpness and Poignancy of Wit exerted
with the greatest Vigor against the *Holy
Order*; in short, Religion and all that is
Sacred, Burlesqu'd and Ridicul'd ; To see
this, I say, and withall, to reflect upon the
fatal Effects which these things have already had, and how much worse are likely to follow, if not timely prevented, cannot but fill the Minds of all good Men
with very dismal Apprehensions.

And are these then the Entertainments

for a Christian to be pleas'd with; for one whose *Salvation* is to be wrought out with Fear and Trembling? Will the Strictnesses of Virtue and Religion be ever relished by a Mind tinctur'd with such Licentious. Representations? Must not such Diversions (to say no worse of 'em) insensibly steal upon the *Affections*, especially of the *Younger sort*; give their Minds quite a wrong Biass, and disarm them of that *Severity* which is their greatest Guard, and which, when once lost, leaves 'em an easie Prey to every Temptation? Will not those *Lewd Scenes* of Love, wherewith almost every Play is fraught, inflame the Fancy, heighten the Imagination, and render a Person thus prepar'd, a fit Subject for ill designing People to work on? But suppose it were possible to be so armed as to be Proof against all these Dangers; yet let any that have the least Regard to what is *Serious*, tell me how they can answer it to *God*, or their own *Consciences*, to be any ways Instrumental towards the *Support* of so much Wickedness? Do they think it a Sin to give the least Encouragement to Vice, and at the same time believe themselves *Innocent*, when by their *Persons*, and their *Purses*, they contribute to the cherishing

rifhing the very *Seed-Plot* of Irreligion?
'Tis to no purpofe for fuch to fay, That they
are cautious what Plays they fee, and always go to the beft; and that the *Play-Houfes* would thrive whether they frequented them or no. This may be true,
but what then, Will this excufe them?
Suppofe a powerful *Rebellion* is begun in
a Nation, and carried on *fuccefsfully*, for fome
time; and a Man fhould not only appear
fometimes among the Rebels, but fhould,
now and then, fend them a *Supply* (tho'
never fo little) of Money and Arms:
Could fuch a one pretend that he was
no ways *Inftrumental* in this Rebellion,
nor Acceffary to the Mifchiefs that attended it, and that becaufe it was not
only *begun*, but would have *profper'd* too,
without him; and altho' he did fometimes appear among the Authors of it,
yet it was with the Party which did the
leaft Mifchief? Do you think, *Madam*,
this a juft way of Reafoning? I dare fay
you do not. Is not this then the very
Cafe I am fpeaking of? Is the *Stage*, as
'tis now manag'd, any thing elfe but a
downright Rebellion againft God and his
Holy Religion? Are not the Plays, (if
not by Defign) yet by a natural and neceffary

ceffary

ceffary Confequence, an *undermining* of his Laws, and an *Attempt* upon his Government? And muft it not then follow, that *every one* that frequents them, is a *Party* in the *Caufe*, and *encourages* the Undertaking? And tho' he fhould be fo Happy as never to fmile at a *Prophane Jeft*, nor join in Applauding a *Vitious* Play; yet, will that exempt him from a Share of that *Guilt* which his Prefence and Purfe has help'd to fupport? No, *Madam*, 'tis *Numbers* ftrengthen the Enemy, and give frefh Courage to his Attempts! A *Full* Houfe is the very *Life* of the Stage, and keeps it in Countenance, whereas *thin Audiences* would, in time, make it dwindle to nothing.

I know, *Madam*, this is ftrange Doctrine to fome People. If a Man talks to them of leaving the Plays, they wonder what he means, and are ready to take him for a Madman. They have fo long habituated themfelves to the *Play-Houfes*, that they begin to think a *Place* there, to be part of their *Birth-Right*: But I defire fuch would be perfwaded to hear what the late A. B. *Tillotfon* thought of thefe matters, (and I hope fome Deference is due to his **Judg-**

Judgment). If they look into the 11*th*
Volume of his *Sermons*, they will find that
in his Difcourfe againft the *Evil of Corrupt
Communication*, he tells them, *That Plays,
as the Stage now is, are intolerable, and not
fit to be permitted in a Civiliz'd, much lefs in
a Chriftian Nation.* They do moft *notorioufly minifter*, fays he, *both to Infidelity
and Vice. By the Prophanenefs of them
they are apt to inftil bad Principles into the
Minds of Men, and to leffen that Awe and
Reverence which all Men ought to have for
God and Religion : and by their Lewdnefs
they teach Vice, and are apt to infect the
Minds of Men, and difpofe them to Lewd
and Diffolute Practices.* And therefore,
fays he, *I do not fee how any Perfon pretending to Sobriety and Virtue, and efpe-
cially to the pure and holy Religion of our
Bleffed Saviour ; can, without great Guilt
and open Contradiction to his Holy Profeffion, be prefent at fuch Lewd and Immodeft Plays, much lefs frequent them, as
too many do, who would yet take it very ill
to be fhut out of the Communion of Chriftians,
as they would moft certainly have been in
the firft and pureft Ages of Chriftianity.*

This

This is the Opinion, *Madam*, of that Excellent Man: and, one would think, it fhould put thofe Perfons who are the Encouragers of Plays, and the Frequenters of them, when they read it, upon an En-quiry, What it is they are doing? Whe-ther they are not carrying on the Defigns of the great Enemy of Mankind? But if that will not prevail upon them, let 'em reflect upon the late Inftance of God's *fevere Difpleafure* againft us, and tell me then, whether they think it confiftent with that *Humiliation* and *Repentance* which this great Judgment ought to awaken in us, and which *Her Majefty*, by Her late Gra-cious *Proclamation*, calls upon us to Exer-cife, to be ever again prefent at a *Place*, where they muft often hear the Name of *God* Prophaned, and every thing that is *Serious* made a Jeft of? .A *Place* which they cannot but know, and muft own, (if put to the Queftion) has contribu-ted fo much to the *Corrupting* the pre-fent Age ; and which, 'tis to be fear'd, is one of thofe *accurfed things,* that has provok'd the Almighty to be fo angry with us.

Thefe

These are things, *Madam*, of no trifling Importance; they are such as deserve the serious Reflections of all *good* Christians, whatever the *Pretenders to Gaiety* may think. And though some may, perhaps, misconstrue and ridicule such Considerations by the Names of *Precifenefs* and *Fanaticifm*; yet, 'tis to be hop'd, that all who have any regard for the *Honour* of God, the *Welfare* of their Countrey, and the *Intereft* of our *Eftablifhed Church*, will not be laugh'd out of their *Duty*, but be perfwaded, not only to withdraw *themfelves* from a Place of so much Danger, but advise *others* to do the like; that the Stage may no longer Triumph in the *Spoils* of Virtue and Religion. 'Tis now the time to begin such an *Undertaking:* We have a powerful Enemy *abroad*, and a more formidable one at *home*; I mean that *Loofenefs* and *Irreligion* which so abounds: and what will it avail us to *fubdue* the one, while we *encourage* the other ? The *Hand of God* has been lifted up againft us, we have feen the *Terrors of the Lord*, and felt the *Arrows of the Almighty*; and what can all this mean, but to awaken us to a due Senfe of our *Danger* ? And, 'tis to be hop'd, hop'd, the Nation has already taken the Alarm, and begin to think how to avert God's Diſpleaſure. The *Stage* is called in Queſtion, and Papers are diſpers'd to warn us of its Miſchiefs; and it is not im-probable that the *Licentious* and *Unbound-ed Liberty* the Players have taken of late years, and particularly in their daring to Act THE TEMPEST within a very few Days after the late dreadful Storm, has rais'd in the Minds of Men ſuch an Abhorrence and Indignation, that we may poſſibly be ſo happy as to ſee the Stage (if not *totally ſuppreſs'd*) yet brought under ſuch a *Regulation*, both as to the *Plays* that are Acted, and the *Company* that Reſort to them, that Foreigners may no longer *ſtand amaz'd* when brought in-to our *Theatres*, nor Good Men *tremble* at the Continuance of them: but that *Virtue* may appear there with all its Charms, and *Vice* be expos'd to the ut-moſt *Contempt*. In ſhort, that the Stage may become ſo *Chaſt*, that even thoſe *Birds of Prey* who now hover about the *Play-Houſes*, and make the Avenues to 'em ſo dangerous, may fly away from a Place that will no longer *Encourage* nor *Protect* them.

But

But after all, *Madam*, Whether this is such a Scheme as can ever be reduc'd to Practice; whether so *noble a Structure* as I am speaking of, can be erected upon so *rotten* a *Foundation*; whether the *Wound* is not *Gangreen'd*, and must be cur'd by *Excision*; I say, whether such a *Regulation* of the *Stage* be possible, must be left to those who have *Skill* and *Authority* to try the Experiment. In the mean time, it will be every one's Duty to run from a Place of such *Infection*, least they contribute to the spreading a *Disease* which may, in time, prove *Fatal* to the whole Nation. But I forget, *Madam*, I am intrenching upon your Patience, while I detain you in a place you have so long abandon'd. I am fallen upon a Subject, which 'tis difficult not to say much of: but I shall no longer interrupt your better Thoughts, than while I beg Pardon for this Trouble, who am,

Jan. 16th.
1704.

Madam,

Your very Humble Servant.

THE
Stage-Beaux tofs'd in a Blanket:
OR,
𝕳𝖞𝖕𝖔𝖈𝖗𝖎𝖘𝖎𝖊 𝕬𝖑𝖆𝖒𝖔𝖉𝖊;
Expos'd in a True Picture of
JERRY *Collier*
- - - - -

A
Pretending Scourge to the *Englifh* Stage.
A
COMEDY.
WITH

A *PROLOGUE* on *Occafional Conformity*;
being a full Explanation of the *Pouffin*
Doctor's Book; and an *EPILOGUE* on
the *Reformers.*

Spoken at the *Theatre-Royal* in *Drury-lane.*
By Thomas Brown.

Simulant Curios, & Bacchanalia vivunt. Juv.

LONDON,
Printed, and Sold by *J. Nutt*, near *Stationers-Hall*, 1704.
Price One Shilling and Six Pence.

Certamen Epiftolare : Or, VIII Letters between an Attorney and a Dead Parfon; Joe
Haines's *Three Letters, being a Supplement to the Second Part of Letters from the Dead
to the Living. Never before Printed. With a Collection of Letters. By Mr.* Thomas
Brown. *Sold by* John Nutt, *near* Stationers-Hall.

This Piece was written by the
author Tom Brown

THE
Epiſtle Dedicatory
TO
Chriſtopher Rich, Eſq;
Patentee of the *Theatre-Royal.*

SIR,

THis Comedy ſeems to challenge a Right to your Patronage, ſince it is a Defence of that Publick Diverſion, at the Head of which you are by the Royal Authority. The Wiſeſt and Beſt People have thought the Stage worthy the Encouragement of the State. Thus it roſe in *Athens,* and grew to that Eſteem, that the State was at greater Expence in the Decorations of it, than in the *Perſian* War. Nay, the Publick Money appropriated to that Uſe was look'd on as a thing ſo Sacred, that ſcarce any Exigence of State wou'd compel them to divert it to any other Uſe.

The Epistle Dedicatory.

In this City the Great *Themistocles* himself was *Choragus*, that is, Super-intendent of the Stage, and took care of the Cloaths, Scenes, and all its other Decorations. The same Post you now are in, Sir, that Great Man discharg'd in *Athens*. In *Rome* the *Ædiles* perform'd what the *Choragi* did in *Athens*, so there it still was under the Inspection of the Magistrate.

Nay, *Milton*, in the midst of the Reign of Enthusiasm and Precisenefs, asserted, That the Pulpit it self wou'd not be more Efficacious than the Stage for the promoting Vertue, &c. And ev'n our Modern Enemy of the *Drama*, Mr. *Collier* has been so fair as to own that Human Wit can't invent a more effectual Way of Advancing Vertue, and Discouraging Vice, by which alone he has destroy'd the greatest part of his Book. But indeed the Stage has no Enemies but such as are Hypocrites and real Enemies to Vertue, because the Stage is a profess'd Enemy to them and their Darling Vices. The Stage exposes Knaves and Fools, Misers, Prodigals, Affectation, Hypocrisie, &c. and that has provok'd some to be its Zealous Foes, under the pretended Name of Sanctity and Religion. Some have pleaded against like Lawyers for their Fees; and that which made them refuse to put in Memorable

In-

Inventions for want of a Two Guinea Bribe, prevail'd with them to Rail and Droll on the Stage, without any real Malice to the Diverfion, but meerly to get a Penny. And thefe Men, if they cou'd hope but a Bribe anfwerable to the Undertaking, wou'd write as much againft the Pulpit, as they have a-gainft the State and the Stage.

There are others who are in effect Enemies of the Stage, who yet pay dear enough for Publick Diverfion, while large Subfcriptions Enrich a fingle Perfon, to the Ruin almoft of that more Rational Entertainment of the *Drama*. But that's a Point too tender to touch upon at prefent, I fhall therefore fay nothing more of it at prefent.

It will be expected, that according to the Mode of Dedications I fhou'd here make a *Panegyric* on your feveral good Qualities ; but I know by that I fhou'd rather Offend than Pleafe you, who are much fonder of doing Good Deeds, than of hearing of them when done. I will not therefore enumerate your Private Acts of Generofity, or Benefits done to Particulars, tho' I eafily cou'd ; but I can't but take notice of thofe from which the Publick derives a Benefit, I mean your Management of the *Theatre*. When under a Pretence

a 2 of

of Liberty there was fo great a Defection, that few but Young Players were left with the Patent, by your Care, and under your Wing, they work'd their Way to the Efteem of the Town, and foon became Powerful Rivals of thofe whofe Eftablifh'd Reputation threaten'd them with Ruin. You have fpar'd no Coft for the Beautifying and Convenience of the *Theatre*, for the Decorations of the Stage, and all things elfe that might improve the Pleafure of the Spectators,

To you therefore this following Play is juftly Dedicated, becaufe it is a Defence of what you have beftowed fo much Time and fo much Money to fupport, and in which you have, as much as was poffible, oblig'd the Town.

I am, Sir, your

moft humble Servant.

Tom Brown

THE

THE
PROLOGUE
ON
Occasional Conformity.

Being a full Explanation of the

Poussin Doctor's Book,

SPOKEN

By One Dress'd One half like a *Noncon Parson,* and the Other like an *Orthodox Divine.*

My *Dress is* odd, *but yet 'tis* Alamode,
  Invented to unite Mammon *with* God.
This Side *is* Real, *and full of* Native SPITE;
This I put on to get some Money *by't.*
This Side *is fill'd with* Sanctify'd Grimace ;   Pointing to each
This is more Debonair *in hopes of* Place.   side alternately.
This Obstinate *against* Religious Forms;
This, brib'd by Gain, OCCASIONALLY CONFORMS.
OCCASIONAL CONFORMING *is our Darling,*
Which if y' *Attaque, you set us* All *a Snarling.*
Pamphlets, Lampoons, full stuff'd with Lies *and* Nonsence,
In Shoals we send abroad in point of Conscience.

How's

The Prologue.

How can it chuse but put our Tribe in Passion,
By HUMANE *Laws* to *be forbid Damnation?*
'Tis an Invasion of the Rights w'inherit;
Damnation *is a Right we claim* in Spirit.
'Tis this that puts us Saints thus all to Work,
To Church Conforming *to set up the* Kirk.
* *Pimps, Preachers, Porters, Pedlers, Weavers, Tinkers,*
Saylors, Coblers, Taylors, and every Sort but Thinkers,
Rhimsters, Atheists, Deists, Whoremasters and Drinkers.
(*For* Kirk, *like Ark of* Noah, *no Beast refuses,*
But takes in All, *tho' for her several Uses.*)
Nay, scarce a MODERATE *Churchman in the Nation,*
Wou'd force us thus upon our Soul's Salvation,
TANTIVY BOYS *alone oppose our dear Damnation.*
A Pox upon their Zeal to save our Souls,
They'd make us Honest, that is, they'd make us Fools.
In vain they give us Liberty of Canting,
If Liberty of getting Gold *be wanting.*
† *A Florid Friend of ours has prov'd of late,*
That POW'R *wou'd make us dreaded by the State,*
Therefore to make us yet more Formidable,
He'd only have Your *Places for* Our ‖ Rabble,
For since the Riches *that we rake won't do,*
He wisely adds your Trusts *and* Places *too,*
Which when we have you need not fear Our *Love,*
For Forty Eight Our *Tenderness will prove,*
When We *like doating* Mothers Nurs'd Your *Church,*
Sure none will *say we left it in the* Lurch!
Or call'd it by hard Names, or seiz'd its Lands,
We *for* Your *Sakes secur'd them in Our Hands.*
We're harmless Lambs, indeed you need not fear us,
Our * *Author proves there is no Mischief near us.*

Like

---

* The Author of *Peace at Home, and War Abroad,* makes the Dissenters to consist of
such a Rabble.   † The foresaid Author of *Peace at Home, and War Abroad.*   ‖ Such
he calls the Dissenters.   *The same.

The Prologue.

Like Gallesp Doves for this dear Pow'r we Stickle,
Meerly, I vow, to save our * Conventicle;
Lawn Sleeves, and Mytres then, with Joy we'll see
In Fundamentals We with You agree.
Ah! Why then will you with Dissenting Brother
About Precedence make so damn'd a Pother?
Give Place to Us, and then you soon shall see
How very Complaisant to You We'll be;
To Neighbouring Scotland turn not thus your Eye.

Thus far in Friendly Guise I'm bid to prove ye,
But if this fail, have other Arts to move ye.
I, like † our Author, imitating Bays,
Come here prepard t'attaque you, Sirs, Two ways,
If mild, beseeching, humble, wheedling, Speeches
Won't gain your Favour——why then—— ‡‡ kiss our B——
(a) We're Rich, and, Sirs, to Riches Pow'r's ne'er wanting,
And since we lose our Point by humble Canting,
We'll try our Bilboes—— or at least our Ranting.
Our (b) Author tells you how far we are able
Once more to turn Paul's Church into a Stable;
And if you thus go on still to provoke us,
Well surely do it, or may the Devil choak us.

The

* They pretend 'tis only to secure the Act of Toleration.   † The Dr.
‡‡ Author of Peace at Home, and War abroad.   (a) This is the Doctor's way
of Arguing, for he first tells us how little is to be apprehended from the Dissenters,
by reason of their mean and low Condition, and then how much we shou'd fear diso-
bliging them for their Wealth and Power; for as if bred in Mr. Collier's School, he
tells us Riches begets not only Consideration, but Power; he puts them in mind, that if
they can't gain their Point by fair Means, they must do it by force; he exhorts them
to Rebellion, and then furnishes them with Reasons, (such as they are) to justifie it.
A worthy Champion of the Church and Religion; and he wisely insinuates the Sincerity of his Zeal for maintaining of Religion, and is urging the Care the State ought
to take of its Preservation, when he is undermining the Religion establish'd in his
Country, by digging down the Fences the Wisdom of the Nation have made about it;
and it is hard to believe, that he who wou'd destroy the National Religion, wou'd
truly promote any: And all those Authors he Animadverts on for Deism, Socinia-
nism, &c. can do less damage to Religion, than he who undermines the Religion of
his Country by a popular Way of advancing its Enemy. Against the first every
one is arm'd, against the latter Men provide no defence, as apprehending no Design of
Invasion.   (b) The same Author.

The Perfons Names.

Urania. { A Lady of Quality and good Senfe, Gay in her Humour, a Lover of Company, and free in her Converfation, of true Honour and Vertue, a Friend of the Stage.

Eliza. { Her Friend and Coufin, fomething more referv'd, and who, tho' fhe love Company, is more Nice in the Choice of it, a Lady of Honour, Senfe, and Religion, a Friend to the Stage.

Dorimant. { A Man of Senfe and found Judgment, Vertue and Honour, of true Morals and Religion; a Friend to the Stage, becaufe it promotes Vertue by expofing Fools, Fops and Knaves.

Hotfpur. { An earneft Foe to Hypocrifie and Coxcombs, a Man of Vertue, Honour, Religion and good Senfe; and a Zealous Friend to the Stage, becaufe it promotes Vertue by expofing Fops and Knaves, &c.

Clemene. { An affected Hypocrite, Coquet, and Jilt, and one whofe Reputation has not been without notorious Blemifhes in the very Eye of the World, and yet continues no Enemy to the Caufe of her loft Reputation, by hoping now to fecure her felf under a noifie railing at Vice, pretends to be a profefs'd Enemy to the Stage fince the Publifhing Mr. Collier's Book, an Admirer of Sir Jerry Witwood.

Lord Vaunt-Title. { Vain of his Quality, a Smatterer in Poetry, who having his Plays refus'd, turns Enemy to the Stage, and condemns the Poets for bringing in Lords fometimes as Fools.

Sir Jerry Witwoud. { A Pert, Talkative, Half-witted, Coxcomb, vain of a very little Learning, always fwims with the Stream of Popular Opinion, a great Cenfurer of Men and Books, always Pofitive, feldom or never in the Right, a Noifie Pretender to Vertue, and an Impudent Pretender to Modefty, a Hypocrite, and falfe Zealot for Religion, and fets up for a Reformer of the Stage, of a Sagacious Nofe, in finding out Smut or Obfcenity; a wonderful Artift at extracting Prophanenefs out of all things that fall into his Hands; a profefs'd Enemy of the Stage, tho' a Frequenter of it; once thought a Divine, but for Reafons beft known to himfelf he has caft his Gown for the Vanities of a Beau Wigg and Sword; Vain, Proud, Ill-natur'd, and incapable of Converfion.

THE

THE
BEAUX
OF THE
STAGE, &c.
A
COMEDY.

ACT I. SCENE I. *A Room.*

Enter Urania *and* Eliza.

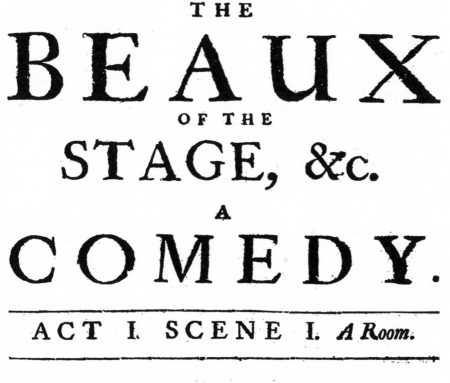

Ura. NO Vifitants yet, Coufin? This is very ftrange.

Eliz. That neither of us have had fo much as one all this while, I confefs is fomething uncommon, when your Houfe is the conftant Rendezvous of all the Young and Gay of the Town.

Ura. I own I have thought the time fince Dinner tedious enough in all Confcience.

B   *Eliz.*

Eliz. To me, on the contrary, it has feem'd extreamly fhort.

Ura. Oh, Coufin! Good Wits love to be alone.

Eliz. Ah, Madam! I'm the Wits very humble Servant, but you know my Pretences to Wit are but very flender.

Ura. The lefs you Pretend the more is your Right, Coufin--- But, for my part I avow my Love of Converfation and Society! Solitude is a kind of Effect of Self-love, and may be excufeable, where there are Beauties to feed the Vanity: But I find fo little in my felf to pleafe my felf, that I'm forc'd to call in the Auxiliaries of good Company to drive away fo unpleafing an Invader.

Eliz. Nay, my good Coufin, I am not fo fmitten with my felf neither, as to be an Enemy of Converfation. Nature has made us for Society, and there's no living without it. And as fhe has made it necessary, fo am I far from thinking it difagreeable: But then I'm for a chofen Company; that which is feleet and pickt, not promifcuous. I hate the Impertinent Vifits of Fools and Fops, of the Crafty, Clofe, and Defigning, of both Sexes, that put us on a painful Guard, and pervert the Pleafure into a Bufinefs: 'Tis that Medley of Company which you receive, that makes it fo pleafing to me to be fometimes alone.

Ura. Your Delicacy is too refin'd, and your Palate too nice, if you can re lifh the Converfation of none but People of Senfe.

Eliz. And your Complaifance too general, that can admit indifferently of all Sorts———

Ura. The Reafonable gratifie my Underftanding, the Fantaftic my Mirth. I relifh the Witty, and laugh at the Fools.

Eliz. A Fool diverts but once, the fecond Vifit muft be naufeous: Who more than once wou'd hear my Lord *Vaunt-Title's* ridiculous Harangues on Quality? Or Sir *Jerry Witwoud's* Awkward Love or Scandal? His Lordfhip's heavy Poetry? Or the Knight's heavier Criticifms?

Ura. On Women, Drefs, and Plays?

Eliz. On the firft he's more fevere, than an old Maid of Sixty, who owes her Celebacy to her loft Reputation; nicer on the fecond than a folemn Coxcomb juft arriv'd from *France*; on the laft more ill-natur'd than an exploded Poetafter.

Ura. Nay, my Lord, and he are Enemies to Women, good Drefs, and Plays, with good Reafon, being laugh'd at by the Ladies, fhunn'd and pointed at by the Men, and expos'd by the Stage.

Eliz. Nay, the Play-houfe, I confefs, they ought to abhor, fince they fo often fee their own ugly Faces there.

Ura. The Stage-glafs is not made to flatter Fools and Knaves, and then for they and their Friends are for breaking the honeft Mirror.

Eliz. Lord! Can't they forbear looking in it, if they are frighted at their own Faces?

Ura. Or can't they correet their Follies, if they find them fo difagreeable?

Eliz. Oh! Never Coufin, never; a Fool is always too fond of his own Judgment, to own his Error by quitting his Folly; and the Knave finds too
much

much the fweet of his Roguery to difcard it, at the expence of his Intereft ; and their real Quarrel to the Stage, is not that it fhows their Pictures deform'd to themfelves, but to every Body elfe.

Ura. I dare fay this is the greateft Pique his Lordfhip, the Knight, and fome others, have to it. Their Follies and Vices are too confpicuous, and too well belov'd, not to engage them in the Squabble.

Eliz. How can you then admit of their Vifits?

Ura. Becaufe every Body elfe does, and I hate to be fingular ; 'tis always the effect of Pride, Ill-nature, or Hypocrifie: Equipage and Title takes away all Blemifhes ; for 'tis only the Poverty of the Fool, or Sinner, not the Folly, or the Guilt, that makes a Fop, or Debauchee, Scandalous, or to be fhunn'd—— Befides, I have order'd my felf to be deny'd, but the familiar things will take no denial. I know no way but making my Footmen turn 'em out of Doors ; and that's a Remedy worfe than the Difeafe——. But why do we prepofteroufly trouble our felves with their Impertinence, when we have the good Fortune to be free from their Vifits ? I wonder *Dorimant* is not come yet, when he promis'd to be here betimes, to give us a Character of the laft New Play, and Sup with us ?

Eliz. Ten to one he has forgot it. Men naturally forget an Appointment : When is the only profpect of the Affignation, the only Vice they are invited to.

Ura. Not Men of *Dorimant's* Senfe and Vertue. *Eliza*, a Man of Senfe, knows there is no Merit in Vice ; and whatever Folly may betray him to the Converfation of the Weak and Difhoneft of our Sex, he eafily finds, that there can be no fure Satisfaction on Friendfhip where there is no Vertue.

Enter Page.

Page. Madam, my Lady *Clemene* is come to wait on your Ladifhip.

Ura. Heav'n forbid ! Ah ! my dear *Eliza*, who can bear this killing Vifit ?

Eliz. A juft Judgment on you, Coufin, for your Complaint of Solitude.

Ura. Run, run down immediately, and tell her I'm not at home.

Page. I have told her already that you are, Madam.

Ura. You heedlefs little Animal you, what have you done ?

Page. Who I, Madam ?

Ura. I'll have you better taught than to give Anfwers on your own Head.

Page. I'll run down and ftop her—— I'll tell her that your Ladifhip is not pleas'd to be at home. [*Going.*

Ura. Stay, you thoughtlefs thing, you—— you've done mifchief enough already.

Page. Why, Madam, 'twill time enough ; for when I came up fhe was engag'd in a Difpute with a Lord, whofe Coach was paffing your Ladifhip's Door when her's ftopp'd.

Ura. Go, get you down, and wait on her up—— Oh ! my *Eliza!* How fhall we fupport the Fatigue of this Vifit ?

Eliz.

Eliz. Nay, I confess the Lady is naturally a little fatiguing, and my Aversion of all Aversions, as *Olivia* says, and I think her (with respect to her Quality be it spoken) one of the most insipid Monsters that ever pretended to Arguing.

Ura. Your Expressions, my Dear, is a little too gross.

Eliz. Not one jot—— No, no—— 'Tis no more than her due; nay, much less, if I did her Justice—— Oh! She's the most intollerable of Impertinents.

Ura. That she most exclaims at.

Eliz. She may exclaim at the Name as much as she pleases, she is most visibly the Thing; for in short she is from Head to Foot the most affected Creature alive; she looks as if her whole Body were out of Joint; her Shoulders, Hips and Head, moving like Clock-work on Springs. She affects a continual Languishment of Vice when she speaks, and is perpetually simpering and rouling her Eyes, to Court the Reputation of a little Mouth and full Eyes.

Ura. St, not so loud—— Shou'd she come up and overhear us——

Eliz. Oh, never fear; she comes not yet—— Her Mind's as affected as her Body; she struggles hard to a Reputation of Wit and Religion, but her Awkwardness betrays her Hypocrisie and Folly: She supplies the Necessities of a Bankrupt Reputation, a Loose Life, with the easie Composition of Noise and Nonsence.

Ura. No more—— I hear her—— I'll receive her at my Chamber Door.

Eliz. But one word, and I've done—— I'd fain have her Marry'd to the Lord we mentioned just now; there's such a near Relation betwixt their Understanding, their Vertue and their Folly, that the Union must needs be extraordinary.

Ura. Hold your Tongue——See, she's here.

Enter Clemene.

Oh, Madam, how long 'tis since——

Clm. Eh! mee Dear excuse me!—— Let me dee if I'm not just dead! Oh! a Chair immediately!

Ura. Page, a Chair quickly.

Clem. Eh ged! Eh ged!

Ura. Ah, Madam! What's the Matter?

Clem. Eh! E'en quite spent!

Ura. What will you have?

Clem. Eh! Eh! My Heart is beating its last!

Ura. The Vapours?

Clem. No, no——

Ura. Will you be unlac'd?

Clem. Eh ged! No—— Eh!

Ura. What's your Distemper?

Eliz. How long have you been ill?

Clem. Eh! I have been above these Three Hours at that filthy Place.—Eh!

Eliz. What

Eliz. What filthy Place, Madam, cou'd your Ladifhip go to?

Clem. I proteft ee'm afham'd to name it————Eh!

Ura. How, Madam!

Clem. Nay, but my Lord *Vaunt-Title*, and Sir *Jerry Witwoud* carry'd me by main force———— Let me dey! It was a perfeft Rape on my Underftanding.

Eliz. Pray, Madam, explain your felf.

Clem. Eh! That School of Debauchery, the Play-houfe, Medem! Let me dey, if I have been there fince the Charming Mr. *Collier's* Book came out, before. And now for my Sins, Madam, for my Sins, was I hurry'd to that Sink of Prophanenefs and Smut———— But it has given me the Palpitation of the Heart fo violently, that let me dey, I fhan't recover it this Fortnight.

Eliz. Ah, Coufin! The Mifery of Humane Life! How ftrangely Difeafes fall on us, which we never dream of!

Clem. And then———— which is the biggeft Misfortune of all, Madam, let me dey, if I did not juft at your Ladifhip's Door meet my Lord *Truewit's* Coach, who on my Complaint had the odious Fally Militate for the hideous beaftly Play-houfe.

Ura. I own, Madam, I don't know what Sort of ftrong Conftitution my Coufin and I are made of, for we were there twice this Week, and yet came home fafe and found, eafie, pleas'd, and gay.

Clem. Eh! Madam, and are you one of the Abandon'd? Do you fee Plays too?

Ura. Yes, and mind 'em too.

Clem. And do they not put you almoft into Convulfions?

Ura. I thank my Stars I'm not fo nice; and for what I can find by Plays, they're more likely to Cure than make us Sick.

Clem. Eh! Madam! What is't you fay? Can any Perfon, that is a Perfon of the leaft Reverence in Underftanding, advance fuch an extravagant Obfurdity? Can a Lady of any feen Parts run fo direftly on the Point and Edge of Reafon, without any Apprehenfion of a———— And is there in reality any Perfon of Senfe, who is fo very hungry and greedy after Laughter, as to be able to relifh the naufeous Impertinencies of Plays? Eh! for mee part, I avow mee infenfible of the leaft grain of Wit in eny of 'em: They all provoke mee in the moft furious Degree of difguft, and ev'n Sicknefs at every thing in them.

Eliz. Ah! With what a charming Eloquence my Lady fpeaks! I fwear I thought a Play a good, innocent, ufeful, Entertainment! But fhe has fo perfuafive an Art, and gives what fhe fays fo agreeable a Turn, that we can't refift our Inclinations to fide with her Opinion.

Ura. I'm not fo full of Complaifance to facrifice my Opinion to another's Humour, without Conviftion: And till I have better Reafons than any of the Party have yet urg'd, I fhall think well of the Stage.

Clem. Eh! let me dey, Medem! if I have not the leaft Pity for you — Eh, take my Opinion mee Dear, and recall the Deviations of your Judgment, let not the World, the cenforious World, know that ever the filchy odious Plays cou'd pleafe you.

Elis.

Eliz. Ah, Coufin! how Gay and Engaging is the very Manner and Air of my Lady's Difcourfe? The very Drefs ravifhes, but the Sence Tranfports. How I pity the poor Players, who have fo powerful an Enemy.

Clem. Eh! the Hideous Obfcenity and Ordures of the Plays.

Ura. Sure, Madam, your Ladifhips Smell has a peculiar turn that Way! For I proteft I can difcover no fuch Matter!

Clem. No, no, mee Dear, you fhall never perfwade me to that—— but you are one of the obftinate Ones, who tho' Convinc'd, think it a Scandal to own your Errour— for let me dey, Medem, if the filthy Poets do not leave the odious Things fo Open and Barefac'd, that there's not fo much as a Lawn Veil drawn over them to juftifie the Beholders, but the beaftly Nudities are fo very Monftrous and Vifible, that the moft proftituted Eyes in the Univerfe can't look that Way without Blufhes and Confufion.

Eliz. Ah! —how many Charms are in my Lady?

Clem. He! he! he! he! he!

Ura. Pray, Madam, be Particular—— point out fome of thefe Ordures, as you call 'em.

Clem. Eh! Madam, is there then a Neceffity of being Particular?

Ura. Yes, where the Cafe is Doubtful.

Clem. Eh!

Ura. Come, pray be Particular.

Clem. Eh! fie!

Ura. I beg you.

Clem. Eh! Madam, you call all the Blood in my Body to my Face! I'm in the laft Confufion, Iv'e not one Word to fay to you!

Ura. I'm Ignorant of the Caufe, being not able to difcover thefe Ordures my felf.

Clem. So much the worfe for you.

Ura. So much the better rather in my Opinion. I only take things to be what they are offer'd for, not give my felf the immodeft Fatigue to Rack and Torture an Expreffion to confefs a guilty Senfe which the Poet neither expos'd to my View, or Meant.

Clem. A Woman's Modefty!

Ura. A Woman's Modefty lyes not in Grimaces and Affectation of knowing more in thofe Particulars than other People; this Affectation is the worft Symptom in the World of a fick Mind; and there can be no Modefty in the World fo Ridiculous as that which takes ev'ry thing in the worft Sence. It difcovers what Hypocrifie wou'd conceal, for it muft argue a very good Acquaintance with the Lady to know her in a Mask and Difguife, and that at firft Sight.

Clem. In fhort, Madam, you may be what you pleafe— but all Plays are full of infupportable Ordures.

Eliz. That's a moft charming Word; Madam, I don't know what it means, yet certainly 'tis the moft ravifhing Word in the World.

Clem. In fine, Madam, you fee your own Coufin takes my part.

Ura:

Ura. Ah! Madam, if you dare believe me, you fhou'd not build much on that, fince fhe's a Diffembler, and won't fpeak her Mind.

Eliz. Oh! fie, Confin— be not fo Mifchievous to bring me into Sufpicion with my Lady! Shou'd fhe give Credit to your Calumny, how Unfortunate fhou'd I be! I hope, Madam, I lye under no fuch injurious Thoughts from your Ladifhip.

Clem. No, no, mee Dear, I mind her not, and believe you more Sincere.

Eliz. Madam, you're infinitely in the Right, and you do me but Juftice when you believe. I think you one of the moft accomplifh'd and engaging Perfons Alive; that I'm entirely vanquifht by your Reafons, am abfolutely of your Sentiments, and extravagantly charm'd with every expreffion you utter.

Clem. Elefe! Madam, I fpeak without Affectation.

Eliz. That's Apparent, Medem! as that all you fay and do is Natural and Eafie, your Words the Tone of your Voice, your Mien, your Actions, your Addrefs, has I know not what of Quality in them, which charms ev'ry Beholder; I'm ftudying every Motion of your Eyes and Mouth; and I'm fo full of you, Medem, that the Town in a little Time will take me for a very Counterfeit of your Ladifhip.

Clem. Eh! Medem! you mock me!

Eliz. How can you think me fo Stupid?

Clem. Let me dey, Medem, I'm but a Scurvy Model.

Eliz. The beft in the World, Medem.

Clem. Eh! You flatter me, mee Dear!

Eliz. Not in the leaft, Medem!

Clem. Spare my Blufhes I conjure you, Medem.

Eliz. Eh! Medem, I've fpar'd you extreamly, for I've not faid a quarter of what I think.

Clem. Eh! Medem! Ged Medem no more —Yo've put me into a moft inexpreffiable Confufion—in fhort, Medem *Urinia,* we are two to one, and Obftinacy and Opiniatietures, you know, are fo unworthy a Woman of Wit,

Enter Lord Vaunt-title *at the Chamber Door ftrugling with the Page, who would ftop him.*

Page. Pray, Sir, go no farther!

Lord. Sure you don't know me!

Page. Yes, my Lord, I do —but you are not to come in.

Lord. What brutal Infolence is this?

Page. My Lord, don't call your Civility in Queftion by forcing into a Lady's Apartment whether fhe will or not.

Lord. I come to wait on your Lady.

Page. But my Lady, Sir, will not be waited on —— I told your Lordfhip that fhe was not within.

Lord. Why, I fee her in the Room there.

Page. That's true, my Lord—— but yet I tell you fhe is not within.

Ura. What's the Matter there?

Lord.

Lord. Only your Ladiſhip's Page is for playing the Fool a little, Madam.

Page. I told my Lord that your Ladiſhip was not at Home, and yet he wou'd needs preſs into the Room.

Ura. And why did you tell my Lord ſo?

Page. Becauſe your Ladiſhip was angry laſt time for letting him know that you were within.

Ura. Was ever ſuch Impudence in ſo Young a Creature! I hope your Lordſhip has a better Opinion of me than to believe what he ſays; he takes your Lordſhip for an Impertinent Dancing-maſter I caution'd him about.

Lord. Oh! Medem, I'm infinitely ſatisfy'd of the Truth of what you ſay, and in Reſpect of your Ladiſhip I ſhall forbear to Teach him to diſtinguiſh better betwixt a Man of Quality and a Dancing-maſter.

Eliz. There's an obliging difference, Couſin!

Ura. A Chair there, Impertinent.

Page. There is one Madam.

Ura. Reach it my Lord.   [*The Page thruſts it rudely to him.*
Lord. Your Page, Medem, has a ſtrange Averſion to my Perſon.

Eliz. He's much in the Wrong, my Lord.

Lord. I fancy my ill Mien is not engaging enough with him, Ha! ha! ha! hey! hey! hey! — But pray Ladies what were you upon?

Ura. The Play-houſe, my Lord.

Lord. I juſt came from it.

Eliz. With this Lady.

Lord. Right, Madam, ſhe did me the Honour to Sacrifice Three Hours to the Adornment of the Boxes: For Rat me if there has not been a Dearth of Beauty there ever ſince her Ladiſhip has forſaken the Houſe, except when your Ladiſhip was there.

Clem. Well, my Lord, your Opinion of the Play-houſe.

Lord. Rat me, a moſt Impertinent Place.

Clem. Eh! How I am Raviſh'd with your Judgment, mee Lord!

Lord. Oh! 'Tis a moſt Abominable Inſipid Place, Rat me, in the Univerſe! Why, Medem, the Devil take me if I was not horribly ſqueez'd to get a Place there! I thought I ſhould have been Smother'd or Preſs'd to Death to get in. See how Hideouſly my Cloaths and Peruque are   and Rumpled : By your Favour, Lady, I muſt adjuſt me.   [*Goes to the Glaſs.*

Eliz. Nay, that indeed ought to cry Vengeance on the Place, and juſtifies your Lordſhip's Cenſure.

Lord. And then the Vulgar Raſcals ſhare with Quality in the Diverſion; the very Footmen in the Upper Gallery will judge of the Plays as well and louder than their Maſters, tho' indeed the Beaſtly things are fit for none elſe to ſee.

Ura. Why how has the Stage offended your Lordſhip?

Lord. Rat me, Medem, the Saucy Rogues that tread it wou'd not Act a Play I wrote for my Diverſion, unleſs I'd ſecure them they ſhould not loſe by it.

Clem.

Clem. That indeed was an infupportable Affront.

Lord. And then, Medem, the Parts are fo impudent fome-times to make a Lord a Fool.

Ura. That's no Reflection on the Lord that has Wit and Senfe.

Lord. Rat me if I wou'd not have them Drubb'd, but that it wou'd coft me Money.

Enter Sir Jerry Witwoud.

Sir Jerry. I beg your Pardon, Madam, for fo late a Vifit: But fince the Play I was hurry'd away by a Couple of Poets of Quality, to hear Two Lampoons, Two Ditties, and fome other Madrigals, which I've forgot already.

Clem. I warrant they were hideous Creatures, Sir *Jerry,* that you cou'd not ftay no longer with 'em.

Sir Jerry. They were the Top of the Extraordinary Private Scribblers, that always communicate their own Writings in a Third Perfon's Name, that they may have the liberty of praifing them the more; and indeed deferve the upper end of all the Coxcombs in Town. Their Poetry was like a Bitch over-ftock'd with Puppies, the Litter of was fo large, that they fuck'd the Senfe to the Skin and Bone. I look upon a Man capable of but Four big Misfortunes— Ill Drefs, no Money, Scribbling without Learning, and Living without a Belly-Paffion; and of thefe Four which do your Ladifhip Think the Three biggeft?

Ura. Oh! The Three firft without difpute, Sir *Jerry.*

Sir Jerry. And of thefe Three were both thefe Sparks moft rampantly guilty: They had the Cacoethes of Scribbling without Learning, Dreffing without Genius, and running in Debt without any Money to pay: It's empty of Wit as a Modern Comedy, as ill Drefs'd as a *Temple* Beaux, and as poor as—as—as a ;Disbanded Enfign, or Colledge Servitor.

Clem. But, Sir *Jerry*, this Company's divided about the Play-houfe, your Opinion may decide the Difpute.

Sir Jerry. The very Mark of the Beaft is on it, 'tis fcandaloufly rampant in Smut and Prophanenefs.

Clem. Do you hear that, Madam? Sir *Jerry* is a Scholar, and he declares for me.

Ura. Opinion and Vogue, Madam, has feldom any force on me, if Reafon be againft them; Reafon and Evidence can never lofe their Excellence, becaufe a Faction run on in a Cry, that has been artfully rais'd by mean Defigns, only to gratifie a Private Gain by a Publick Injury.

Sir Jerry. Madam, when I fay it, you may fatisfie your felf I have Reafons enough for my Affertion.

Enter Dorimant.

Ura. Oh! *Dorimant*, you are come to my Affiftance in a lucky Minute, and bring Right, a better Advocate than a Woman.

Dor. Not than fuch a Woman as your Ladifhip, Madam: But I pray Ladies and Gentlemen keep your Places, nor let me interrupt your Difcourfe, for you are on a Subject that has long divided the Town.

Ura. Here's my Lord's a violent Enemy of the Stage.

Lord. True, Medem, I am fo——— for it's Contempt of Quality. In fhort, it is a moft deteftable Place; refufe me, deteftable to the laft Degree; more deteftable than any thing that can be call'd deteftable.

Dor. My Judgment and Reafon then are moft deteftable.

Lord. Why, rat me, *Dorimant*, doft thou pretend to defend it?

Dor. Yes, my Lord, I am that bold Man——— But pray, my Lord, what are the Reafons of your Indignation?

Lord. Reafons why the Stage is deteftable?

Dor. Yes, my Lord.

Lord. It

Lord. It is deteftable, becaufe it is deteftable.

Dor. After this indeed, who wou'd fay one word more—— The Sentence is paft, and the Pulpit without any more ado condemn'd.

Lord. Sir *Jerry* here's of my mind.

Dor. The Authority is admirable, I confefs.

Sir Jerry. And are you a Defender of the Stage?

Dor. Certainly, Sir *Jerry.*

Lord. Demme, I'll take care to inform the poor Rogues of their Advocate. Hay! hay! He, he, he!

Clem. Eh! Let me dey, Mr. *Dorimant,* this is furioufly incongruous to your Reputation!—— for Mr. *Collier* has prov'd the Poets a Company of ftrange debauch'd Fellows— who are furioufly my Averfion.

Dor. Mr. *Collier* does by the Poets, what he fays *Ariftopha- nes* did by *Socrates,* he puts them on an odious Drefs, and then Rails at 'em for their Habit. But what fay you if I am perfuaded to be for the Stage, even by your beloved Mr. *Collier?*

Clem. }
Lord. } He! he! he! That's pleafant indeed!
Sir Jer. }

Clem. Eh! Mr. *Dorimant,* you are for Paradoxes to fhew your Wit!

Dor. I am for Truth, Madam— and what I fay I give my Reafon for—— He tells us in the very Front of his Book, That the Bufinefs of the Stage is to Recommend Vertue, and Difcountenance Vice, to fhow the Uncertainty of Humane Greatnefs, the Sudden Turns of Fate, and the Unhappy Conclufions of Violence and Injuftice, to expofe the Sin- gularities of Pride and Fancy, to make Folly and Falfhood Contemptible, and to bring every thing that is Ill under Infamy and Neglect. After this, who wou'd not be for the Stage, that dares pretend to be a Lover of either Vertue or Senfe?

Sir Jerry.

Sir Jerry. But you forget his Cloud of Authorities against it.

Dor. Authorities! Against what, Sir *Jerry?* Against the most efficacious Means the Wit of Man can invent for the Promoting Vertue, and Discouraging Vice? What signifies Authorities against Reason? But he has omitted some things which our Stage does of equal Value with what is mentioned——It ridicules Hypocrisie and Avarice; the first ruining Religion, the latter the State; so that the Stage is the Champion of the Church and State, against the Invasions of Two of their most formidable Enemies; and this is what renders it odious to those who cry out against it. It is not that it is Lewd, Prophane, or Immoral; but because it exposes the Vices and Follies of a too prevailing Party, the Hypocrites, and Misers.

Clem. Eh! Ged! Mr. *Dorimant,* and don't you think that the Stage is guilty of Smut, Prophaneness, and Blasphemy?

Dor. I think some Poets have been guilty of some of these Faults, but from a Particular to a General there is no Arguing. And the *Goliah* Adversary of the Stage wou'd not allow it in his own Case, because there has been Prophaneness and Blasphemy in some Particular Pulpits, therefore the Pulpits is Prophane and Blasphemous. But I shou'd be tedious to say all I cou'd from your Chief Stage Accuser.

Clem. Eh! Sir, pray go on——Sey all you have to say—and then have the Mortification, let me dey, to see that one Line of Mr. *Collier* is more prevailing than all your Harangues——

Dor. Ah! Madam——I'm ready to sacrifice my Reason to your Opinion, and make the Stage submit to your Resentment without one word more in its Defence——

Clem. Eh! Ged! Mr. *Dorimant,* you're too Complaisant——No, no, take your own Sentiment, I wou'd not owe my Victory to my Eyes, but my Reason.

Eliz.

Eliz. No, no,— me Ledy is more Spiritual, Mr. *Dorimant;* you'll find it a hard matter me Ledee or me.

Dor. Why, Madam, how long have you been of her Opinion?

Eliz. My Lady here by her admirable Reasons and engaging Manner has won me to her side since this Difpute began, therefore I'll have no Private Parley with the Foe—But fince my Lord and I have not much to fay in the Controverfie, we have the better Opportunity of Converfing on a more agreeable Subject.

Clem. Lerd, Madam, me Lord indeed is a perfect Mafter of the Art of Love.

Eliz. Your Ladifhip fpeaks fenfibly of his Lordfhip's Perfections—But I affure you, Medem, his Lordfhip's Quality is to me much the more agreeable Entertainment.

Lord. Nay, the World does me the Juftice to own that no Man fhows more of the Port of a Perfon of Quality, or can fay more in Defence of it againft the Damn'd Levelling Part of the Tawn——

Enter Page.

Page. Madam, Supper's on the Table.

Lord. Oh Lerd, Medem, your Ladifhip's humble Servant.
[*Going.*

Ura. By no means, my Lord, if you'll be pleas'd to fhare a fmall Collation, you'll do me a peculiar Honour : 'Tis a perfect Ambign, and Word of Ceremony, fo I befeech your Lordfhip to make none to go to it.

Lord. Your Ladifhip's Command, Madam, is enough for your humble Servant: Refufe me——

Ura. Come, my Lady *Clemene,* we'll fhow the way ; and before we part I hope Mr. *Dorimant* and I fhall be able to bring you to a more favourable Conftruction of the Stage and its Friends.

Clem.

Clem. Eh! Ged, Medem, name not the Sage, unless you design to save your Supper; for let me dey if it be not a perfect Vomit to Chaste Ears!

Sir Jerry. Madam, when we come to Order and Method, you shall see me throw this positive Knight on his Back, or I'll never enter the Lists again.

Dor. Be not so confident of Victory, that often leaves you too open to your Adversaries Thrusts. But the Town is already almost come off from your Court.

> *Fancy a while may please the giddy Town,*
> *With that false Reasons may a while go down:*
> *But when at last their fading Beauties fall,*
> *Right Reason then and Justice will prevail.—*

The End of the First Act.

A C T II.

Enter Lord Vaunt-Title, Dorimant, *and* Hotspur.

Lord Vaunt. DEmme, *Dorimant,* if I ever saw a Fellow so
baffled in my Life, tho' *Hotspur* here came to
his Affiftance; not one word to fay for thy felf, refufe me,
Ha! ha! ha! he! he! he!

Hotfp. You may laugh, my Lord, as much as you pleafe,
but 'tis not the goodnefs of your Caufe that engages
your Mirth, but a poor Refuge of baffled Argument;
when the Fool can do nothing with his Underftanding, he
wou'd confound you with Noife.

Lord Vaunt. You are very free, Mr.———

Hotfp. I fpeak not of your Lordfhip, but of abundance of
the Patrons of his Book, who when they have not Judgment
enough to difcover the weaknefs of the Reafoning, run it up
with a more ridiculous Mirth than the Author is guilty of
in the Buffoon Part. " Oh! There's abundance of Wit in
" the Book, 'tis very pleafant, and fo with a fcurvy Jeft on
" the Poets they march off with an imaginary Triumph.

Dor. But admitting (what I do not grant) that the brisk
Pertnefs of the Author were true Wit, what has that to
do in a Subject of that import which he fuppofes this to
be? If the Corruption of the Morals of the Age depend
on it, or the Encouragement of Vertue, few Points can be
advanc'd

advanc'd which requires a more ſerious Conſideration. Now 'tis not probable that Men ſhou'd think him in earneſt when they ſee him ſo merry; not that his Reaſons be ſo clear and plain, while deliver'd in the midſt of Buffoonry and Laughter: *And Laughing and Eſteem are ſeldom beſtow'd on the ſame Object,* as he himſelf obſerves, *p.* 26. of his *Defence.*

Lord Vaunt. I know not what you may think, *Dorimant,* but in my Opinion he ſeems entirely Maſter of his Argument.

Hotſp. Why truly he uſes it as if he were, for he often gives it away.

Lord Vaunt. Oh! Good Mr. *Hotſpur,* you are witty, but that will not confound Reaſon; this is falling into the Vice you condemn.

Hotſp. By no means, if I do it in the midſt of an Argument, if I confound my Reaſoning with my Mirth, and blend Fancy and Judgment ſo diſproportionably, that the reliſh of the former wholly ſwallows up the latter, then I am guilty of his Fault, who mingles ſo much falſe Rhetorick with his ill Reaſoning, that 'tis evident Truth was the laſt of his Thoughts, and the leaſt of his Aim. But I underſtand not what you mean by being Maſter of his Argument, unleſs contradicting himſelf be to ſhew his Maſtery of it.

Enter Urania, Eliza, Clemene, *and Sir* Jerry Witwoud.

Clem. He! Cavaliers, let me dey if you are not the moſt unpoliſh'd that ever were admitted to the Converſation of Women of Quality! What, run away before us? I proteſt, had not the Complaiſant Sir *Jerry Witwood* been here we had been left all alone, let me dey, which had been furiouſly incongruous.

Ura. Oh! Madam, while you were with us we cou'd never be alone.

Clem.

Clem. Oh! Never fay it, Madam, all Women without a Man is furiously infipid; the biggeft Misfortune can befal us: And that you, my Lord, fhou'd be guilty of fuch a Solecifm among Ladies!

Lord Vaunt. Refufe me, Madam, if thefe Fellows did not hurry me away with the heat of the Argument, till I had quite forgot my Duty to your Ladifhip. But I am the moft confounded Perfon that ever was guilty of an Offence againft the Fair.

Hotfp. You that are a Wit, Madam, and a Lady of Argument too, will fure excufe the Fault the Defence of your beloved *Collier* betray'd him to.

Clem. Alas! I can forgive any thing for that dear Man's fake; but all that can be faid againft him is very trifling; let me dey, he has baffled all the great Wits of the *Stage*, and muft be invincible to all his leffer Foes.

Sir Jerry. Your Ladifhip fpeaks like an Oracle; only more plain and more true; and 'tis not that I think *Dorimant* or *Hotfpur* can convince me, but 'tis the hopes of my convincing them, that I engage in the Difpute.

Clem. If Reafon wou'd do, their Party, let me dey, had been long fince convinc'd, but for meer fterility in Argument, they grow Scurrilous.

Ura. fo indeed Mr. *Collier's* Friends fay.

Clem. And, Madam, don't your Ladifhip think the Amendments too full of Reflections, and thofe, let me dey, too rude and fevere?

Ura. And don't your Ladifhip, Madam, think Mr. *Collier* too full of Reflections, and thofe too rude and fevere?

Hotfp. Is not he the Aggreffor? Has he us'd the Poets like Gentlemen?

Dor. Or like Chriftians? Has he not call'd them Blafphemers, Irreligious Buffoons, &c.

Ura. Nay, has he not deny'd them worthy to come into the Church? And what more Scurrilous and *Billingfgate* can come

D   from

from any Pen, than what almoft every Page of his Book is full of?

Dor. And yet with Reverence to Mr. *Collier*, fome of the Gentlemen he has us'd fo abufively are Men of Candour and Honefty.

Hotfp. And as good, if not better, Chriftians than himfelf, and worthy to enter any Church but his.

Dor. And after this, can thofe who are provok'd by him, be blam'd for ufing him as ill as he has them, without any Provocation at all?

Hotfp. And tho' he fets up for a peculiar Excellence of Life, Principle, and Practice, his Second Book fhews that he is not very good at bearing a Repartee; for through the whole Piece his Anger is vifible enough.

Sir Jerry. Come, Gentlemen, you may fay what you pleafe, but Mr. *Collier's* Book is not Scurrilous; he is in a heat, but 'tis againft wicked Men; if they will take it to themfelves, they are to blame, not he.

Hotfp. That is indeed his weak Plea in his *Vindication,* but his Reflections in that Book are at leaft particular; and when he himfelf coins the Wickednefs he rails at, he is to blame, not thofe who find his railing immediately directed to them and their Works; but perhaps his Party think it an invading Mr. *Collier's* Property, and will have *Scurrility* his peculiar Prerogative; and as he can difcover Smut and Prophanenefs where other People can find nothing of the Matter, fo that the Terms of Exorcifing his own *Devils* are entirely in his Power.

Sir Jerry. Why, Gentlemen, are you not really convinc'd by what has been urg'd againft the *Obfcenity* of the Stage?

Hotfp. The Queftion might with more Juftice be put to you.

Sir Jerry. And you don't think the Stage really guilty of *Profanenefs?*

Hotfp. Lefs than of *Immodefty.*

Lord.

Lord. Refufe me, thou art a moft incorrigible Fellow, *Jack*, ha! ha! he! I warrant there is no fwearing nor curfing on the Stage? Ha! ha! he!

Sir Jerry. Ay, my Lord, no fwearing: Ha! ha! he!

Clem. O! Swearing is furioufly my Averfion, I can't endure the found of an Oath, it makes me ftart! Let me dey, Madam, if an Oath does not difmantle all the Fortifications of my Underftanding, and leaves my Mind for the time a heap of Confufion. Why a Soldier's Oath is as frightful to me as the Report of his Piftol.

Dor. Ah! Madam! What have you faid? What fhock our Ears with fo fmutty an Expreffion? Modefty is the Character of your Sex, and to talk out of that is to talk out of Character. A Soldier's Piftol! O hideous!

Clem. Alas! I fee no harm in the Expreffion, let me dey!

Dor. Nor I in moft that Mr. *Collier* has directed us carefully to in his *Chapter of Immodefty*: Yet you find, like another *Columbus*, he has made the wonderful Difcovery of ftrange *Ordures*, as your Ladifhip calls 'em; and the Frolick is defign'd to be carry'd round, the Ladies words are to be drawn into the fame Premunire, till in their own Defence they are reduc'd to *utter Silence*, and fo Mr *Collier's* Character of the Sex maintain'd to the rigid extremity.

Clem. Ah! But the charming Mr. *Collier* does not mean that they fhou'd be filent any where but on the Stage, where the fcandalous, ill-bred, Fellows, the *Poets*, let me dey! make us fpeak fuch filthy things, that I cou'd love——

Dor. Oh! Fie, Madam; there again! *Love!* Why, did not all the Ancient Poets keep clear of *Love?* And are not all Mr. *Collier's* Darts fhot againft the *Butt* of *Love?*

Clem. Not againft Innocent *Platonic Love*, Mr. *Dorimant.*

Hotfp. Oh! Pardon me, Madam, the Name it felf is infamous, and contains all the ugly Ideas of things that muft not be thought of, as Toying, Kiffes, Vows, and Oaths of Conftancy and Fidelity, Enjoyments, Quarrels, Revenge,

Billet

Billet Deux, Intrigues, and so forth. O, name not *Love,* if
you wou'd not for ever disoblige Mr. *Collier.*

Eliz. This is running the thing to Extravagance.

Ura. And so is most of Mr. *Collier's* Constructions of
Immodesty and *Prophaneness.*

Dor. As you shall see, Madam, before we part yet.

Sir Jerry. " What is more frequent than prophane Cur-
" sing and Swearing, and the Abuse of Religion and Holy
" Scripture ? They wish one another at the Devil ; they
" imprecate all the Curses, all the Plagues and Confusion in
" the World, to one another ; then they swear by all Things ;
" and all Persons swear, of all Degrees and Qualifications,
" on all Occasions, in Love, and in Quarrels, in Success
" and Disappointments, &c. and this, I think, is both a-
" gainst Religion and the Law.

Hotsp. None of the Instances produced by Mr. *Collier* are
forbid either by the Law or the Gospel.

Sir Jerry. " Thirdly, 'tis Ungentleman-like, as well as
" Unchristian ; the Ladies compose a great part of the Au-
" dience, and to swear before them is to frighten 'em. The
" Second Branch————.

Hotsp. Nay, before you come to the Second Branch, let us
cut off the First.

Clem. Why sure, Mr. *Hotspur,* you can deny nothing of
this Charge ! Let me dey, the Words are plain enough in
this particular.

Hotsp. I think not, Madam ; I think the Words are quite
contrary, and so far from being *plain Oaths,* that they are
plainly no Oaths. First, by the Intention, and next, by the
Words themselves. The Intention is plainly against Mr. *Collier.* For these Mock-Oaths, as some call 'em, were contriv'd
on purpose to avoid swearing, and to supply the vehemence
which is natural to a Passion, or earnest Asseveration, without
the guilt of an Oath ; and these in the Latin and other
Languages are call'd *Adverbs,* and *Interjections ;* and I think
                                                        what-

whatever a thoughtlefs Company of People may fay to the contrary, that thofe Words made ufe of by the Poets to avoid fwearing, may very properly be call'd fo in ours.

Dor. Mr. *Collier*, and all Divines of the Church of *England* that have writ on this Subject, allow of *Moral Reprefentations*. Now not to be abus'd and impos'd on by Words, a *Moral Reprefentation* fignifies the Reprefentation of the Life and Actions of Man, exprefs'd in the various Manners of his feveral Ages, Conditions aud Paffions; by that to fet before our Eyes a true and juft Picture of our Follies and Vices, as well as our Vertues, that having no Intereft or Concern in the Perfons reprefented, we may make an Impartial Judgment of the true Merit of Folly and Vice, and the Excellence of Vertue, being then the moft capable of judging when our Mind is moft divefted of *Favour* or *Intereft*.

Ura. Oaths, I think, are generally the effect of Paffion, and fpoken with Noife and Heat; and I find from what both you and Mr. *Collier* have faid, that if the Paffions are at all to be reprefented, they are to be reprefented truly, and therefore the Poets to keep Nature, and at the fame time not to be loofe, or offend Religion and Good Manners, form Sounds that may fupply the vehemence of Paffion.

Dor. Your Ladifhip comprehends the Matter. The Heathen Poets fwore at length, and without referve, nor were they, in my Opinion, to blame at all for it; for fwearing was not only the Natural and Common Language of the Paffions on fome Occafions, but it was to them no Crime to fwear out of their Plays: But with us the Cafe is alter'd, and as it is a Sin in Common Life, fo 'tis avoided by the Poets in their Reprefentations.

Lord. Nay, the Poets, rat me, fwear in cold Blood, without the excufe of Paffion, on Confiderations, and in their Clofet.

Hotfp.

Hotſp. Your Lordſhip has borrowed that extraordinary Remark from Mr. *Collier*, and therefore as his, not your Lordſhips, I muſt needs ſay 'tis one of the moſt Childiſh and Trifling in his Book ; and that's a bold Word: For Mr. *Collier* knows very well that the Poet is here but as it were the Hiſtorian, he only ſets down the Actions, Paſſions and Words, of others, not his own ; and he might as well ſay that the Sacred Author of the Scripture curs'd with *Shimei*, as that the Poet ſwears with the Perſon that is introduced by him: Nor is it in cold Blood, for whoever writes a Paſſion truly, is poſſeſs'd by it, and then the Poet can't be ſaid to ſwear in cold Blood.

Dor. That is ſuppoſing there are Oaths in the Plays, but that is plainly denied by the Poets ; and when the Ingenious Author of the *Relapſe* had confuted him in this Particular, in bringing Parallel Inſtances out of the *French*, which are fully as much, if not more, Oaths, than thoſe of Gad, Icod, Gadſooks, &c. and aſſured us that Perſons of the niceſt Converſation, moſt refin'd Morals, and Religious up to the height of Bigottry, uſe them, and thoſe not only of the Laity, but even the Clergy themſelves, and that one wou'd think ſhou'd juſtifie it with Mr. *Collier* ; but he is reſolv'd to yield nothing, tho' never ſo evident ; anſwers very rationally— *There is no arguing from the Practice to the lawfulneſs of it.* But by his leave there is ; when the thing in Diſpute is not evident, the Practice of Good, Pious, Religious, and Scrupulous, Men is a very ſtrong Argument and Demonſtration, that theſe Good, Pious, and Religious, Perſons do not think this daily Practice an ill thing ; and the concurring Approbation of ſo many Men of this Character is a ſufficient Confutation of the Caprice of one Whimſical Cavillier againſt it.

Sir Jerry. But the Caſe is not the ſame, there is none of the *French* Mock-Oaths but *Par Die* that comes near it.

Hotſp.

Hotfp. Sir *Jerry*, you and your Namefake have a notable way with you to impofe on the Common Senfe of all the World ; is not *Mort Bleu* as near the Sound and Orthography too of *Mort Dieu*, as I-cod is to the Oath by G— Is not *Me Foy* as much an Oath as *I-faith ?* What Oath does *Codsfifb* bear any likenefs to ?

Dor. But let the likenefs be never fo great, 'tis evident 'tis not the fame, for the difference of one Letter alters the Senfe of a Thoufand Words, as in *than* and *then,* the Sign of the Comparative Degree and *Time, gilt,* and *gelt, Horfe,* and *Herfe,* and fo on. Thus *Gad* is no more *God,* than *than* is *then, gilt, gelt, Horfe, Herfe,* &c. The defign of the Word in its firft formation and conftant ufe is purpofely to avoid the latter Senfe, and this is the only way of coming to the proper Senfe of a Word when the meaning of it becomes dubious, and in difpute, as the meaning of thefe Words are now.

Ura. 'Tis true, Mr. *Collier,* who generally has peculiar Notions of things different from the reft of the World, may perhaps mean and think of God when he pronounces thefe Words ; but I dare ingage for all Men befides who fpeak it, that they have no fuch Thoughts.

Dor. And the Poets ufe it on purpofe to keep that awful Refpect that is due to the Holy Name, appropriated to the firft tremendous Caufe of all Things, the Source of Goodnefs, and the Preferver of Mankind. If this be impious, and againft Law, 'tis he is the Offender, not the Poets.

Sir Jerry. But do not the Perfons in the Play fwear by Heaven ! Can you have any Evafion of that too, for I find you are prepar'd againft moft of our Objections?

Dor. If the fame be among Chriftians, I think it fhou'd be avoided only for the fcandalizing the Weak ; but if among Heathens, I do not think it fo heinous ; and in both Cafes I take the Poet to be inculpable, fince he only draws from the Practice of the World, and not from any peculiar and proper inclination to fwearing.   *Hotfp.*

Hotfp. Next I wou'd defire to know if the Scripture be to be taken in the very ftrictnefs of the Letter ? Then the Quakers are in the Right ; but if it be lawful to call Heaven, nay, the God of Heaven, to witnefs in a petty Squabble betwixt a couple of Whores, in their Trials in the moft Petty Courts in the Kingdom, nay, for the proof of the leaft Intereft of Half a Crown, I can fee no Reafon why in the Atteftations of our Honourable Love to a Vertuous and Worthy Object, we may not call Heaven to witnefs the Sincerity and Reality of our Intentions, if what we affert be true; and if this be lawful or inoffenfive in Life, it is no lefs fo in the Reprefentation of Life.

Lord. Ah! *Hotfpur,* thy *Spur* is cold now ; is that the beft Anfwer you have ? He! he! he! he! he!

Hotfp. I confefs, my Lord, 'tis the beft I have at prefent ; and, I think, none of the moft defpicable neither: I fhall at leaft continue in that Opinion till I fee better Reafons to convince me than any Mr. *Collier* or his Favourers have yet brought. As for the offence to the Ladies, 'tis only a Childifh Flourifh of Mr. *Collier's* Rhetorick, and not worth taking any notice of.

Dor. Therefore your other Divifion of the firft Branch, *viz.* CURSING. That is alfo the effect of *Paffion,* and if it be lawful to Reprefent the *Paffions,* may be lawfully brought into the *Drama. Job* is fet us in the *Holy Writ* as an Example of Patience, and of a Good Man, and therefore from his Conduct we may gather at leaft thus much, how far it is lawful to make a Reprefentation of the Paffions of Men ; for while we keep within this Model, we cannot err.

Sir Jerry. What, do you compare the infpired Writings of the *Holy Ghoft* to the paultry bufinefs of the Stage?

Dor. By no means —— but I fay, that as the Scripture is the Rule of our Life, fo I can perceive no Fault in making it the Rule of our Writings too, which are of more import
than

than our Private Actions. And since in some part of the Holy Writ the meanest Actions of Life, and e'en of the Wicked, are Recorded, I suppose it will be no Fault to justifie our own Performances by that.

Hotsp. Besides, Sir, by yours and Mr. *Collier's* leave, the Business of the Stage is not so paultry a Concern as he is pleas'd to call it : Can that be paultry whose Business 'tis to encourage Vertue, and discountenance Vice, to shew the uncertainty of Humane Grandeur, to expose the Singularities of Pride ? &c. Your Party I confess is not without their trifling Evasions to pretend this Book not Answer'd. If the Author be Easie, Genteel and Witty, like the *Vindicators of the Relapse*, &c. then 'tis *Banter*. If it be mixt with just Repartees, admirable Reflections, like the *Amendments*, then 'tis Scurrilous. If like others, the Matter be seriously and plainly handl'd with sound Reasoning, then 'tis Dull.

Dor. Nay, to do Mr. *Collier* and his Friends Justice, their Measures are Politily taken ; to make sure Work on't there's nothing like charging the thing home, attacking the Stage in those that are the Support of it, in the Author's and in the Ladies, to tell these that it is injurious to their Modesty, Religion and Vertue.

Ura. Not considering that it is at the same time to charge all the Ladies with a notorious and publick *Breach* of their *Modesty, Religion* and *Vertue*, in frequenting those very *Plays* he Arraigns.

Dor. Or at least that they are not so sagacious in discovering Smut, as Mr. *Collier* ; and a Vicious Imagination may blot a great deal of Paper at this rate with ease enough.

Hotsp. Nay, but Customary Swearing takes away the Sense of doing it, and I'm afraid it may be applicable to other Matters, says Mr. *Collier, Defence, p.* 98. Now this reaches all these Ladies that have not yet, or did not then, discover what

E   Mr. *Collier*

Mr. *Collier* has fince done in thefe Matters; a pretty kind of Anfwer, thus when he is charg'd with wrefting and turning the Words, to make them fignifie what the Poet never meant, nor does plainly exprefs, then he returns, that it's the Poet's Cuftomary fwearing or writing *Smut* takes away their Senfe of it.

Dor. On the contrary, 'tis as Mr. *Congreve* obferves, a familiarity with bad Idea's, that brings them on every the leaft occafion to his view.

Ura. That feems to me to be like the reft of his Arguments and Anfwers. He is charg'd with perverting and mifconftruing every thing, or at leaft every thing that he Quotes; he has Anfwered nothing to this but a plain denial, and meerly fays, that fince the Poets Crimes are too black to name, they pretend Innocence; never reflecting that thefe general Charges, and unprov'd Affertions, will hold for and againft every one, the moft *Innocent*, as well as the moft *Guilty*, and can be therefore of no Force.

Dor. But then to fay that Men are guilty of Crimes that are not to be nam'd, is meerly faying fo, and downright *Billingfgate* Scandal; and his Caution in this is extremely ridiculous and whimfical; for where is the difference betwixt quoting the Paffages, and pointing to 'em in the Plays themfelves, ev'n to the Scene and Page, unlefs it be to gratifie the Bookfellers, by ftirring up the Criminal Curiofity of People whofe Fancy turns that way to buy the Plays, and find out the Myftery?

Clem. How can you Treat Mr. *Collier* fo feverely, when he only followed the Dictates of his Confcience?

Lord Vaunt. Your Ladifhip is directly in the right, Medem, his Confcience fet him on work; well, I'll make him my Chaplain.

Dor. Ah! my Lord, have a care of that, for he will be then your Mafter; a Chaplain is Servant to none but God, as he tells you : And as for his Confcience I dare fay he has not Affurance enough folemnly to affert that it fet him to work.

Sir Jerry. Pardon me, Sir, for he fays, *That being con-vinc'd that nothing has gone farther in debauching the Age than the Stage-Poets and Play-houfe, I cou'd not employ my Time better than in writing againft them,* &c.

Hotfp. Convinc'd? By what? Fifty Pounds? The only Argument that will hold Water; for all he has produc'd are meer Words; and he might have found fome other Caufes of Debauchery more dangerous, and more worth his true Zeal, as being real, and not meerly imaginary.

Clem. Eh! Let me dey, fay what you will, Mr. *Collier* has prov'd the Poets a Company of ftrange debauch'd Fellows, who are moft furioufly my Averfion.

Dor. Mr. *Collier* does by the Poets what he fays *Arifto-phanes* did by *Socrates*, he puts them on an odious Drefs, and then rails at them for their Habit, which I think fomething unfair on Mr. *Collier's* Part.

Sir Jerry. *On the contrary I conceive it ex-* Preface to the *treamly defenfible to difarm an Adverfary, if* Defence of the *it may be, and difable him from doing Mifchief;* Short View. *to expofe that which wou'd expofe Religion, is a warrantable way of Reprizals; thofe who paint for Debauchery, fhou'd have the* Fucus *pull'd off, and the coarfenefs underneath dif-cover'd. The Poets*——

Hotfp. Good Synonimous Sir *Jerry,* not fo faft; firft, who made the Poets his Adverfaries but himfelf? And firft to abufe a Man, and then to fteal away his Sword falfly, and with treachery, is not fo defenfible neither. To tell the World firft, that Men of Candour, Honefty, and Generous Principles, as I know Mr. *Congreve* to be, are Lewd, Prophane, Blafphemous, and Immoral; and after that to go on and tell the World too that they are a Company of Fools to take 'em for Men of Wit, and

Poets,

Poets, is what none but Mr. *Collier* fhou'd do with fo bare-fac'd an Affurance, and thefe Sort of Reprizals are not fo warrantable as he imagines.

Ura. He fhou'd firft fairly have quoted the whole and full Sayings of each Author, have fix'd an undoubted Standard of Obfcenity, Prophanenefs, and Blafphemy, and then have evidently demonftrated that the Paffages he Cenfur'd fell immediately under thofe Heads; for Crimes of that deep Dye fhou'd not be charg'd lightly on any Man, and much lefs on Men of unqueftionable Reputation: 'Tis the greateft Murder that can be committed, and a Calumny that, without Repentance, in my Opinion, calls as heavy Judgments on the Offender as any.

Clem. And do not you then think the Stage guilty of Smut, Prophanenefs, and Blafphemy?

Ura. I do not deny but that there are Plays which are guilty of fome of the Charge; but thofe Mr. *Collier* has not been pleas'd to mention, till the Preface to his laft Book, where he touches on fome that are guilty of one Part of his Accufation: But from the Proofs of his firft Book there is no concluding in Mr. *Collier's* Favour.

Dor. A Charge of this Nature ought to be *clear*, the Proof *ftrong*, the Evidence *unqueftionable*, the Matter of Fact *vifible* and *plain*, to all Men that hear it. But on the contrary, no Body, (to give one Inftance for all) till Mr. *Collier*, e'er thought that Saying of *Valentine* taken from Scripture, or that Mr. *Congreve* put the Perfon and Words of our Bleffed Saviour into the Mouth of a Madman; had this been plain, or cou'd it have enter'd into the Heads of the Senfible and Religious Part of the Audience, it wou'd have been hifs'd off the Stage; the Poet has declar'd he never meant it, and the Audience evidently never perceiv'd it, and yet Mr. *Collier* is not fatisfy'd.

Hotfp.

Hotſp. Nay, I dare avow that there are not Ten People in any Audience but wou'd have been ſhock'd at the Blaſphemy; and driven the Actor off the Stage. On the contrary, I ſaw it often my ſelf, with ſeveral Pious and Religious Friends of mine, and it never enter'd into our Heads to imagine any ſuch thing.

Dor. Nor mine, nor any Man's, that ever ſaw or read the Play, I dare affirm, but one of Mr. *Collier's* looſe Principles, who can be guilty of arrogating to himſelf a Righteouſneſs above all Men, as well as a Judgment and Senſe Superior to all the Men of Wit in Town: But that what I urg'd but now is true, *viz. That it wou'd have been hiſs'd off the Stage*, is evident from this one (inſtead of many) Inſtance, that Expreſſion in the *Relapſe*, hinted at by the Author in his Preface, for barely having a ſuſpicious Face, and looking a little too rudely on the Clergy, was not borne by the Audience, and therefore left out the ſecond Night. And one ſmutty Song in a late Play provok'd the Audience ſo much, that the Merit of the Play in general cou'd not retrieve the good Fortune that had robb'd the Author of. The *Soldier's Fortune*, The *Little Thief* of *Fletcher*, (whom Mr. *Collier* juſtifies) The *London Cuckolds*, and ſome others of that Lewd Stamp, are never frequented by the *Boxes*, or the better part of the *Pit.* Where there are real Faults, either in *Religion* or *Morals*, the Audience is nice and diſcerning enough to find them out, and accordingly diſcourage the Author; but where the Fault is ſo obſcure, that it wants an Interpreter to diſcover it, 'tis the Scrutineer, not the Poet, is guilty; ſince where-ever there are Words that bear a double meaning, (and ſome Induſtrious Men in that way will force a double meaning on very ſimple Words) the beſt and moſt innocent ought to be, and is, taken by the juſt Reader or Hearer.

Sir Jerry.

Sir Jerry. Well, well, let Mr. *Collier* have been never so severe, I think he has Reason; and as he says, *The Poets are the Aggreſſors, let them lay down their Arms firſt; We have ſuffer'd under Silence a great while; if We are in any Fault,'tis becauſe We began with them no ſooner.*

Hotſp. We? What *We?* How comes Mr. *Collier* to write in the Royal Style? But if he mean by *We* the Clergy of the *Church of England,* he joins with his *Scotch* Brother, the Doubty Author of *The Stage Condemn'd,* and juſtifies all that *He* has writ againſt it; and which, next to the *Perſwaſive to Conſideration,* is one of the moſt Impudent and Scurrilous Libels that was ever Publiſh'd in any Government againſt ſo Awful a Body of Men, and a Church Eſtabliſh'd by the known Laws of the Nation.

Dor. Now if the writing againſt the *Stage* be a Duty incumbent on the Clergy, then it muſt be own'd, that Mr. *Collier,* and the Stage Condemner, are in the right of it; and Dr. *Gentiles,* Dr. *Caſe,* Dr. *Gager,* Eminent Divines of that Church, the whole, or at leaſt the major and governing part, of the Clergy, with King *Charles* I. at their Head, have been infinitely in the wrong.

Clem. Yes, yes, 'tis a ſhame to be ſpoken, the Clergy have been too much the Encouragers of the *Stage*; but the Clergy are a Sort of Spiritual Fathers, and we know the Curſe of *Cham.* Yet I think the Divine that tranſlated Father *Caſſaw* extreamly to blame, when Mr. *Collier* had writ againſt the *Stage.*

Hotſp. So ſays the *Stage-Condemner*; but if Priority of writing gave a Juſtice to the Cauſe, Dr. *Gager,* Dr. *Gentiles,* &c. bring the right to the *Stage,* and put Mr. *Collier* in the wrong Box.

Sir Jerry. But if Mr. *Collier* be in the wrong, you are not to correct him: Shall they correct the Church who are not worthy to come into it?

Dor. I

Dor. I am secure however, since I have Mr. *Collier's* good Friend, the *Stage-Condemner,* on my side; for if he may abuse the whole Body of the Clergy, I hope I may oppose one eloping Member.

Clem. But you and the rest of the Stage-Advocates have dealt too rudely with him, considering his Character, let me dey!

Hotsp. By no means, Madam, for when he has laid aside the Dignity of his Gown, for the *Jingle* of a *Pun*; the *Modesty* and *Charity* of his Profession, for Publick *Slander* and *Abuse*; the *Gravity* of his Character, for the pert Railery of a *Buffoon*; he denies himself (the only Mark of his Christian Self-denial) the Reverence that shou'd be paid him; by his own Example he has taught them to be Abusive, and as to him Consecrated *Scurrility.* When his Gown is laid aside, and we find him on the Pad to Rob People of their Reputations, 'tis but just to serve him as his Assault deserves; and you know *'tis extreamly defensible to disarm the Adversary, if it may be, and disable him from doing Mischief*——*Those who paint for Debauchery, shou'd have the* Fucus *pull'd off, and the coarseness underneath disver'd.*

Lord Vaunt. Refuse me, *Dorimant,* the Poets are monstrously oblig'd to thee, thou putt'st in for the next Fawning Dedication, Demme! He! he! he! he! he!

Dor. 'Tis Pretty visible to any Reader that will but impartially survey his Two Books; and his *Defence* in particular makes it most evident that his Aim is not *Truth,* but Victory; that his Quarrel is Personal; that he wou'd amuse the Fancy, not inform the Judgment; and that if he get by the Copy, he is not much concern'd whether the Cause he defends be good or bad.

Hotsp. Right, for if his Aim had been sincerely the *Truth,* and the pure Advantage of Religion and *Morals,* he wou'd never run into affected Repartees, angry Recriminations,

criminations, and malicious Infinuations, againſt thoſe who defended themſelves againſt his abuſive Calumnies, and at the ſame time avoid or ſlur over the moſt Material and Fundamental Points unanſwered.

Ura. And catch at every little Overſight that may afford him but a wretched *Witticiſm:* (For Example, he is tranſported ſo much againſt Mr. *Congreve* (an Argument he is ſomething touch'd with his Amendments) that he tells him, *That he has ſaid nothing comparable to* Ben. Johnſon, *nor perhaps never will.*

Hotſp. Beſides the little Maliſe of the Reflection, there is not *Engliſh* in it, nor never are Two Negatives. But this by way of Parentheſis. He follows not the Conduct of Men of a ſincere Intention, who are always convinc'd before by a ſerious and thorough Diſquiſition of what they wou'd perſuade the World to.

Sir Jerry. But, Lord, Gentlemen, how Paſſion carries away your Judgment; you ſeem to find Fault with the Pleaſantry of the Book, which was the only Means he cou'd think of to make his Book ſpread and pleaſe, in order to do that Good he deſign'd it ſhou'd; had he made a dry, jejune, Argument againſt the Stage, the generality of Readers wou'd never have look'd into it; the Favourers of the Stage eſpecially wou'd have thrown it aſide as all *Sermon* and *Cant:* But now he has by a plentiful mixture of *Wit* made his Book *Diverting,* as well as *Inſtructive.*

Hotſp. But he quits the *Inſtruction* for the *Diverſion;* he aims at the diſguiſing a *falſe Reaſon,* and a falſe Thought, in a briſk Expreſſion; or perpetually to vary the Dreſs of one and the ſame thing till the Judgment of the Common Reader is confounded. 'Tis his omitting true Reaſoning, not his ſprinklings of his Darling Buffoonry, that I Anſwer; tho' I confeſs he is driven to a neceſſity of it by a bad Cauſe, and a ſcarcity of true Reaſon.   *Dor.*

Dor. Befides, tho' the Bulk of his Book wou'd not have been fo big, yet there is *Medium* enough betwixt *Dulnefs* and *Buffoonry, Cant* and *Chriftian Philofophy,* to have gain'd the Caufe, if *Truth, plain Truth* and *Religion,* had been his Aim.

Hotfp. And he may affure himfelf (if his apparent Pride op-pofe not fuch a Piece of Humility) that 'tis neither the Ju-ftice of his Caufe, nor the Force of his Reafons, that has promoted the Sale of his Books; but the Merry Scandal and Drollery they are fill'd with; 'tis not the Di-vine, or Reafoner, but the Buffoon, that pleafes.

Sir Jerry. Pray be particular, Sir, in your Charge; Words you know. Butter no Cabbage.

Lord Vaunt. Ay, ay, come, Sir, be particular; refufe me, I love to be particular, *Dorimant*—— he! he! he! he!

Dor. To give all the Inftances his Book affords wou'd be tedious, a few fhall fuffice; he catches at a trifling Miftake of Mr. *Dennis's* about *Plutarch,* but at the fame time takes no notice of the very material Contradiction charg'd on him by the fame Author in his *Introduction* to the fame Book; and chufes rather to leffen the Credit of his Op-pofer, than juftifie himfelf in fo Fundamental a Point, on which the whole Controverfie turns; for 'tis not whether there be any Prophane, Immodeft, or Blafphemous, Expref-fions in one or more Plays, but whether any Plays at all be lawful or not.

Hotfp. True— for in the very opening of his Book he tells us the admirable ufe of the *Drama,* than which no-thing in Nature can be of more Weight and Confidera-tion with the honeft Part of Mankind.

Ura. And at the end of his Book he fpends a whole Chapter to prove that there ought to be no *Plays at all.*

Dor. And were that true, all the foregoing Part of his Book, and all thofe Books he feems to defign on the fame Subject, are fuperfluous, and only to enlarge the Book, and

F   puzzle

puzzle the Cause, by meddling with Matter foreign to his Business; to divide and extend the Controversie to an endless Confusion; to divert the Dispute from the General and Primary Point, to a meer Particular, Personal, Abuse and Squabble.

Hotsp. This not only we, but the Authors who have writ, has charg'd Mr. *Collier* with, and which he ought in the first place to clear himself of; and of much greater importance than any thing in his *Vindication*; I mean if his Aim be *Truth*, and the *Benefit of Mankind*, and not his own particular Profit in spinning out a Dispute that wou'd else fall within much a narrower Compass; and which being put into a fair and honest Light, the World would be the more capable of judging of the Merits of the Cause. 'Tis this is what Justice and Honesty too call on Mr. *Collier* for; and which if he passes over still thus calmly, we must conclude his Aim's *Mercenary*, that he seeks any thing rather than *Truth*, and that the good of the People is the last of his Considerations. In fine, he must either abjure his *Introduction*, or destroy his *Conclusion*, since they are diametrically oppos'd. This is no trifling Part of the Controversie, but the ground, the bottom, of the whole.

Dor. The charging particular Sayings in the Poets with *Smut*, *Prophaneness*, &c. first is nothing to the *Stage* in general; next to prove ev'n that Charge, you must first agree on a just *Standard* or *Definition*; else it will be right *Rabby Busie* and the *Poppet* indeed, as it has hitherto been. For in all Disputes the Terms ought to be clear and adequate, to avoid Cavils and endless Squabbles about *Words*, and *inextricable Obscurity*. This was told Mr. *Collier* at the first appearance of his first Book; but he finds it Safer, and more to his Purpose, to go on in the *General Obscurity* of the Word, than to bring his beloved *Smut*, *Prophaneness*, &c. to any *known Standard*.

Hotsp.

Hotsp. He is charg'd with Miscitations, False Constructions, and forcing False Meanings on other Mens Words, but is far from thinking it worth his while to disprove the Charge; he takes no notice of the Quotation he made out of *Ben. Johnson's Discoveries*, Patch'd up of Two different Places, and the middle, which alter'd the meaning, entirely left out. He only says he has *not* forc'd the meaning of the Poets; and when he shou'd prove what the Author of the *Relapse* produces of *Bull's* Speech guilty of *Smut*, he only says he fears he shou'd disoblige the Reader by endeavouring of it.

Dor. And he is in the right on't, for by his nauseous Comment he must have discover'd how far he is read in the *Language of the Brothels*, and with how much ease he cou'd pervert the plain and obvious meaning of the Words, when no Body but himself can discover any tendency to *Smut* or *Prophaneness* in them.

Hotsp. That indeed is the way never to be convinc'd; and after this what wou'd it signifie to shew his False Representations of Things, his Misconstructions, or his False Reasoning; you are convinc'd of his Excellence, and will be convinc'd of it right or wrong.

Sir Jer. That may be the Case with some of the Friends of the Book, but not with my Lady, Mr. *Hotspur*, she has irrefragable Arguments for her Opinion, and therefore is not within the Verge of your Reflection. Mr. *Collier's* Acquaintance with the Ancients is too visible to be deny'd.

Hotsp. True, I own it so visible that his Talent of Misrepresenting can't be hid here too. He brings the Ancients to condemn the Moderns, and at the same time excepts the only Poet extant that is a Parallel to the Moderns; if they are guilty of his Accusation, *Aristophanes* is so visibly guilty of Obscenity, that as Mr. *Congreve* has observ'd, he names things directly, which none of the Moderns do, a double Entendre being their highest Crime;

F 2   but

but by his way of Arguing the Moderns muft be more Criminal than the Ancients; becaufe he, as he calls it, he cuts off *Ariftophanes*; had there been more Greek Comic Poets extant, he wou'd have done the fame with them, and then his Argument had been juft in this manner; The Moderns are more guilty of *Smut* than the Ancients, if you take away all the Ancients that are guilty of *Smut*. This is the real force of all he has faid about *Ariftophanes* in that Chapter, and this is his way of Arguing. Can this convince or pleafe any but Children? For the Argument is much more forceable thus, *Ariftophanes* is very Obfcene, and he writ but after the Mode of the Age, therefore to judge of what is not extant, by what is, the Ancients were much more guilty of Obfcenity than the Moderns.

Sir Jerry. But there is no Arguing from Heathenifm to Chriftianity.

Hotfp. Why does Mr. *Collier* do fo then? If his Inftances are nothing to the purpofe, why are they produc'd? I'm fure 'tis plain he urg'd them to prove the *Novelty* and *Singularity* of the Modern Poets Tranfgreffion in feveral Particulars; but if they prove quite the contrary to what he produc'd them for, fhall he immediately caft 'em off, and fay there is no Arguing from Paganifm to Chriftianity.

Ura. It proves at leaft this undeniably, that his Calumny is a falfe Charge, and that the Moderns are not fo culpable as the Ancients.

Lord Vaunt. But you fee, refufe me, that he has prov'd *Ariftophanes* an Atheift, and a prophane Fellow; and if you are fond of his being of your Party, rat me, you may have him, he! he! he! he!

Ura. To fee, my Lord, how things may be mifreprefented, I have read Mr. *Rymer's* Books of Criticifms, and he a Man fully as well acquainted with the Ancients, as Mr. *Collier ller* in the Opinion of the Town ; and he gives us a quite contrary Image of *Ariftophanes* ; he makes him a Man of Merit, a Man of a bold and undaunted Vertue, who purfu'd Vice where-ever it was, either in the greateft Statef-man, General, Poet, Orator, or Philofopher ; that he kept Pride, Self-defigns, and the Ambitious Machinations of the Great Men of *Athens,* in Bonds, in Awe, and fo was the Guardian of the Safety and Service of the Common-wealth, and that the wholfome Liberty of the Stage in thefe Particulars was Silenc'd by the Arbitrary Law of the Thirty Tyrants ; (but that may be the Caufe Mr. *Collier* is fo fond of that Law) and then for his Charge of Atheifm, Mr. *Rymer* will tell you that he was only for the expofing the Folly of the Plurality of the *Athenian* Gods, which was the fame Caufe for which *Socrates* dy'd.

Clem. Eh ! Medem, this is furioufly contradictory, when Mr. *Collier* tells you that he accus'd or expos'd *Socrates* only for his Belief of the Unity of the Godhead.

Dor. But, Madam, Mr. *Collier's* Affertion is of no force, when we know that the Abufe of *Socrates* proceeded from a Private Quarrel, not that Opinion ; and that Revenge made *Ariftophanes* take hold of the Popular Opinion to compafs what he aim'd at.

Lord Vaunt. A good Argument, refufe me, for the Ho-nefty of the Man.

Hotfp. I will not fay much in Juftification of the Action, becaufe I find Mr. *Collier* makes ufe of the fame againft the Poets, who being profefs'd Enemies to *Vice,* to *Hy-pocrifie* and Sedition, he makes ufe of the Artifice of *Legerdemain* to make them appear Blafphemous, Lovers and Promoters of Obfcenity, Prophanenefs and Immorality ; juft *Ariftophanes* againft *Socrates.*

Dor. But the *Greek* Poet has the Advantage of the *En-glifh* Divine, the Matter of Fact was true, and *Socrates* was
guilty

guilty according to the Law of that Country ; but the Poets are abfolutely innocent of the greateft part of the Charge.

Ura. Nay, his Pique to his Countrymen is very remarkable, he can fpeak of *Euripides*'s calling Whoring Stupidinefs and Folly, but overfee Old *Acafte's* Advice to his Sons, and *Chamont's* Advice to his Sifter, in the *Orphan*, on the fame Subject, befides a whole Volume to that purpofe, which might be Collected out of our Modern Plays.

Dor. Nay, Mr. *Collier* has forgot what his beloved *Euripides* (who was indeed a great Man) tells him, *That he that praifes the Cuftoms and Manners of another Country, is no Friend to his own.*

Hotfp. But when a Man of Mr. *Collier*'s Judgment can extol *Euripides* only for barely calling Whoring *Stupidnefs* and *playing the Fool*, and at the fame time rail at and abufe his own Countrymen for giving a more emphatic Demonftration of that Maxim, by fhewing the Truth of it by Examples, making every one fee it plainly by its Inquietudes, Hypocrifies, Quarrels, Profufion, and Ruin of both Reputation and Eftates; what fhall we fay of his Honefty, as tender a Point as he thinks it?

Ura. Right, can any one fee *Dorimant* (as engaging as Mr. *Collier* may think his Character) fo Falfe, fo Fickle, to quit immediately the Woman he has undone, forfake and abufe *Loveit*, who was paffionately fond of him, and no fooner enjoy *Belinda*, but leave her, and not plainly and obvioufly reflect on the Folly of Surrendring to a Man of the Town, and quitting our Vertue for fo frail and fhort-liv'd a Satisfaction, which muft inevitably lofe us what we defire, and which nothing but our Vertue can retain. And thus again in Mrs. *Fondlewife* (tho' the Poet has at laft indeed, as it were, brought her off with her Husband) are not all the Fatigues, the Difquiets, the Frights, the Difcoveries, and the Ingratitude,

and

and Infidelity of her Gallant, fufficient to deter any Woman of Common Senfe from being falfe to her Husband ; and is not her Character a juft Warning and Reproof to any Man of fuch a difproportionable Age, to have a care of Marrying any Woman of fo much Youth, without a good Affurance of her Vertue ?

Dor. But to make the Cafe more plain, let us but fuppofe what is common ; a Woman innocent enough in her Nature, tho' frail or uncapable of refifting the Temptation of Curiofity and Love join'd together, prefs'd by the engaging *Wit*, Artifice, and Perfon of a handfom young Libertine, that has regard to nothing but his own immediate Satisfaction, fpares no Vows, no Oaths of Conftancy and Love, (which yet he thinks no more of) no Method, nor cunning Art of Perfuafion to fteal on the Heart and Affections of a young innocent Lady, unpractic'd and unskill'd in the Common Falfities of Common Men, hoping the Truth and Reality of their Vows, confiding in their fworn Sincerity and Secrecy, tir'd perhaps with the Morofenefs of an old, and incited by the Blandifhments of a new, Lover, fhe yields without knowing the Danger. Then too late fhe finds the Ills fhe did not forefee, and wifhes in vain that fhe had been forewarn'd of the Infidelity of the Young Wild Fellows of the Town, the Evils of an unlawful Amour, and how falfe and fleeting the empty Enjoyments of Vice always prove. Then fhe comes too late to the Play-houfe, and only fees with Sorrow what, if feen before, wou'd have forewarn'd her wavering Refolutions, and prevented her Ruin. And thefe Affairs the more lively and truly they are drawn, the more touching, and of the greater Ufe, they are.

Hotfp. But this is not the only Vice and Folly the Stage reproves and expofes. Had he read the *Virtuofo*, he wou'd have found a Character, a juft Reflection on which wou'd have done him fome good, and have prevented

vented him, like Sir *Formal*, from haranguing it so often on a Moufe-trap; and never have labour'd for the Flourifhes of a falfe Rhetoric, and the Sophifms of a falfe Reafoning, to obfcure the *Truth*, and amufe and confound the Common Reader. Who but he cou'd read the *Plain Dealer*, and quarrel with fome Affronts to his peculiar Modefty, and never mention the numerous and admirable Inftructions of the Place, from whence there is fcarce any thing relating either to our Conduct or Honefty, but may be learn'd, not only from the excellent Reflections through the whole Play, but by the very *Characters, Plot, Moral*, of the Play it felf.

Dor. Oh! Mr. *Collier* is us'd to that Sort of Dealing, he Quotes the Life of *Euripides* in Mr. *Barns's* Edition for one thing that he thinks makes for him, but takes no notice of all that may make againft him.

Sir Jerry. Why, no Man is oblig'd to furnifh his Adverfary with Arguments againft himfelf.

Dor. Not if he Argues for Arguing fake, as 'tis more than probable that Mr. *Collier* does; but if *Truth*, Sir, the *Naked Truth* and Honefty, be his Aim, no Argument ought to be pafs'd over unclear'd which make for the contrary Pofition, which he has done both in *Ben. Johnfon's Difcoveries* and here.

Hotfp. But not to lofe the foregoing Argument till a little farther clearing and juftifying faulty Characters, which will anfwer great part of his Book, were his Objections real, not imaginary, I wou'd ask him whether the Vices reprefented on the Stage are not in the Practice of the World?

Eliza. No doubt of it.

Hotfp. There are then Tempters of the Chaftity of Wives and Maids, whofe Principles are loofe, whofe Love falfe, and Defigns meerly felfifh, and many of thefe Men of a Sprightly Addrefs, whofe Wit impofes on the weaknefs of them that liften to 'em; now to fhew this

juft

juft as it happens in the World is the Poet's Duty, by
that Means to warn the Ladies of the danger of their
Converfation, who might elfe be won by their Falfe
Vows, and ill apply'd Wit. But when on the faithful
Picture of the *Drama* they obferve that there are Men
of Wit, who want Judgment enough to embrace Vertue,
make no more than a wretched ill-natur'd Jeft of a
Woman's undoing, it muft of neceffity arm them againft
the powerful Temptation.

Ura. For my part I have feen many Plays, and defign
to fee many more, very well acted, but never found any
of thofe Effects Mr. *Collier* charges on the *Stage*; nay, in
all my Converfation and Acquaintance I cou'd never
meet with any one individual Perfon that receiv'd thofe
ftrange Impreffions. I have indeed feen Tears drawn
from the Eyes of both Men and Women, but that cou'd
have no ill Effect on their *Morals*; I have feen Laughter provok'd by *Comedy*, and Mirth is what St. *James* himfelf allows. I have known feveral come away from a
good *Tragedy* with Pious Refolutions, and a Contempt of
the World, of Ambition and falfe Glory, which were fub-
ject to fuch fudden Overturns; but never heard of any
that either loft or weaken'd their Vertue by the hearing
or feeing a Play.

Dor. But fhou'd there be a falfe Inftance produc'd, the
ftrange perverfnefs of the Nature of One or Two is no
Proof againft us, fince fome will turn the moft whole-
fome Food to crude and noxious Humours, by reafon of
a bad and corrupt Digeftion.

Ura. Nay, I am abfolutely convinc'd that (excepting fome
few Expreffions, and fome few Plays) the Stage is not bad, but
mifreprefented. Nay, if the Bufinefs of Plays be what Mr.
Collier tells us in the Introduction to his firft Book, it is,
or ought to be, the moft vallid Place next the Pulpit;

for our fecond Duty is Morality ; and if we muft believe him againft it, muft we not believe him for it?

Dor. Nor has he clear'd the Point in his *Defence*, a-
bout the *Athalia* of *Racine*, that if it were not defign'd
for the Stage, he has nothing to object ; for Madam
Maintenon's Reclufes, if we believe fome printed Accounts,
are not fo Innocent but the Stage Ladies may cope with
them for their Vertue ; and 'tis certain moft of the fame
People, at leaft the Court Part of it, make up the Audience
of one and the other. Now in Common Acceptation, *ex-
eat aula qui volet effe pius*, let him leave the Court that
wou'd be Pious, is what will fet the other Part of the
Theatre Audience on as good a Bottom as the Court ;
thus there being no Moral nor Real Evil in the Boards,
Brick, Stone, Paintings, *&c.* in the Publick Theatre above
the Private Stage, and the Audience being the fame, or at
leaft as Religious and Good, his Exception about *Athalia's* being defign'd for the Stage, remains ftill as foolifh
as ever.

Ura. Well, Madam, I hope this has fo far convinc'd
you, that you will not be fuch an utter Foe to the Play-
houfe as you have been of late.

Sir Jerry. Madam, when your Partifans here will talk
all, and hear nothing, 'tis no wonder they gain their
Point, at leaft in their own Opinion.

Clem. And you really think the *Stage* is not guilty of
what he charges on it.

Dor. That fome particular Plays are fo 'tis not to be
queftion'd, but what is that to the *Stage* in general ? Confult
the *Evangelian Armatam*, and you'll find a good number of
Sermons full of *Blafphemy*, but will you argue from thence
that the *Pulpit* in general is *Blafphemous* ? Yet this is
all the force of Mr. *Collier's* References ; fome particular
Plays in fome particular Places are *Smutty*, therefore the
Stage is fo.

Hotfp.

Hotfp. Nay, and which is yet more ridiculous, to bring ev'n that Truth into queftion, he has under all the Heads quoted what is only *wrefted* to an ill meaning, without being *really* guilty of it.

Sir Jerry. Well, I fhall fee Mr. *Collier* in a Day or Two, and I'll give him the Sum of what you have faid on this Point, and I am pretty fure he'll be of my Mind, that you have not clear'd the *Stage*, or anfwer'd his Charge.

Dor. I will not believe fo ill of his Senfe as to think him incapable, being convinc'd by Evidence; but I confefs, I can eafily, from what he has done already, believe that his Honefty, as *tender* as he calls it, will let him deny his Conviction, feek out fome trifling Cavils, return fome malicious Infinuations, and fo with Scandal evade the force of the Argument, and make work for a new Book, which is fure to bring him in 50 or 100 Guineas from the *Hypocritical Party*, befides his Copy-Money.

Lord Vaunt. Rat me, *Dorimant*, 'tis a fign of a baffled Caufe when you grow Scurrilous.

Dor. My Lord, the Refult of his Publick Works is no *Scurrilous Reflection.* When a Man thinks it does not concern his Reputation and Honour to write *directly* and *clearly* for the TRUTH, 'tis no Crime to tell him fo in plain Words.

Ura. Come, come, my Lady *Clemene*, you fhall not deny me, the *Relapfe* is play'd to Morrow, and we will all go fee it, and then we fhall judge the better of the Juftice of the Remarks, I'll fend my Servant to befpeak Places immediately.

Clem. Eh! fye, Medem, let me dey if the very Thoughts of it do not put me into a kind of Convulfions. Eh! Ged, name not the Play-houfe.

Ura. Why, Madam, I have known you a very great frequenter of the Boxes in that very Play-houſe you're now ſo averſe to?

Clem. Ah! Medem, revive not my Misfortune, my Infamy.

Eliz. Nay, Couſin, don't receive my Infamy too.

Clem. But indeed this I may ſay for my paſt Foible in that particular, I did not perceive any *Smut*, any *Immodeſty*, *Prophaneneſs* or *Irreligion*, in the Plays at that time. Wou'd your Ladiſhip believe it, Medem? Let me dey if I did not ſee thoſe very Plays that are now ſo furiouſly odious to me with all the Innocence in the World. Nay, ſo blind was I, that I did not perceive the leaſt of theſe horrid Crimes in any of them.

Sir Jerry. Cuſtomary Swearing you know, Madam, takes away the ſenſe of it.

Clem. But let me dey, Medem, I had no ſooner read this Divine Man's Book, but I turn'd immediately to the Plays which I bought for that End, and found all he ſaid true to a tittle, ſo much did he open my Eyes, and cure my Blindneſs! Eh! Medem, his Book preſently clear'd my Underſtanding, ſharpen'd my Apprehenſion, and enlarg'd my Fancy; for I found it all *Smut*, all *Prophaneneſs*, and *Immorality*, too groſs to blot his Lilly-white Paper with.

Ura. Is it poſſible, Madam!

Clem. Eh! Ged, Medem, let me dey if he be not a moſt Charming Man at diſcovering *Smut* and Ordures; there is not his Fellow in the Univerſe: Believe me, Medem, I have experienc'd it not once, but ſeveral times.

Dor. How, Madam! Several times, after you were convinc'd that it was Obſcene?

Clem. Oh! Yes, Mr. *Dorimant*, I read it once to ſee whether it were ſo or not; and finding it ſo, I read it again to be confirm'd that I was not miſtaken; and a
third

third time to be fure that I advanc'd nothing but Truth when I defended his Judgment in Obfcenity ; and a fourth.

Eliz. Oh! Good Madam, for what? A fourth fay you?

Clem. Yes, a fourth, to raife my Indignation againft the Poets, and wonder at the Ladies that yet frequented their Performances ; and a fifth time——

Ura. Oh! Madam, for God's fake no more, or you. give me Convulfions too in my turn!

Clem. Why, do you think Mr. *Collier* read them but once over? No, no, he is too perfect in them all not, to have read them over, and over, and over again, and again too. And let me tell you, you may read them over as often as you pleafe, if it be with a good intent, to fortifie yonr Averfion to the Prophane Stage.

Hotfp. But, Madam, if you may read 'em fo often for that End, why may you not fee them as often for the fame End?

Clem. O Lard! Sir, no feeing, I befeech you! Lard, to fee the beaftly things ; no, no, I have left off feeing *Smut* and *Prophanenefs*, let me dey!

Ura. I fwear, Madam, you are fomething extraordinary, and fingular in your apprehenfion of things.

Clem. Eh! Medem, not fo fingular neither——I'm not the only Lady that has forfaken the Play-houfe on the reading Mr. *Collier's* Book: There's Mrs. *Trifle* and her whole Family, her Five Daughters and all, who never us'd to mifs a good Play, have on this Account entirely abdicated the Play-houfe.

Hotfp. Pray, Madam, why?

Clem. Becaufe, as Mr. *Collier* fhews you, the beaftly Poets fill their Plays with abominable Ordures.

Ura. And cou'd not they and your Ladifhip, who are of fo very nice a Smell, and fingularity in Vertue and Religion, find out this before Mr. *Collier's* Book came out?

Clem.

Clem. I have told you that they pafs'd unheeded; let me dey, I now wonder at our Stupidity.

Ura. If your Imaginary *Ordures* were not fo vifible as to be difcover'd by all thofe Women of the niceft Vertue and Senfe, who come to Plays, nay, who encourag'd thefe very Plays, and do yet frequent them, and fay yet that they cannot make thofe Infamous Difcoveries in them, 'tis a fign that the Stage is not fo guilty as is pretended; for where there is any honeft-meaning in the bare Words, 'tis the *Hearer*, or fuch *Reader* as Mr. *Collier*, that create the Ordures and Criminal Smell.

Dor. If there be a double Entendre, why, Madam, will you and your Friend put us to the Blufh by taking away the innocent Garment, and fetting naked before us the guilty Signification.

Clem. Phee! Mr. *Dorimant*, whenever there is a double Meaning, care is taken to fet the worft fide of the Expreffion to the Audience.

Hotfp. By Mr. *Collier*, indeed, who points you to fuch and fuch Places, and tells you there is Obfcenity enough, if your Imagination will but affift you in the difcovery.

Ura. But, Madam, were that care you fpeak of taken either by the Poet or the Player, then it muft always have been too vifible for the Ladies of Vertue and Honour (who by frequenting encourage thefe Plays) not to difcover it; and thus Mr. *Collier* is pleas'd to bring in all the Ladies of Quality and Vertue guilty of favouring a known lewd Diverfion, which is a Rudenefs as Brutal as the Calumny is Falfe, and yet the certain and inevitable Confequence of what both you and Mr. *Collier* affert; and this is the Court he awkwardly makes to the Ladies in behalf of his Book. For to deny that thefe Plays were encourag'd by the Ladies of Vertue and Honour, as well as Quality, and by them frequented, is to

deny

deny daily Matter of Fact, of which there are a Thousand
Witnesses.

Dor. But to say that these Places were *not* visible and
obvious before Mr. *Collier*'s Book of *Strange Discoveries,*
is to grant, that the Accusation is not so evident, the
Crimes not so plain, as is pretended by him and his
Abettors; that they were never before taken in that
lewd Sense he is now pleas'd to give them; and by consequence, that not the Poets, but the Reformer, is guilty
of *Immodesty* and *Smut,* &c.

Hotsp. And, I think, that any Lady, who on his Book
(which is so distinct from Truth and Evidence) forsakes the
Diversion of the Play-house, plainly and shamelessly confesses that she saw all this before, and was delighted
with the nauseous Entertainment, while it remain'd a
Secret, and *unmask'd*; but the luscious Feast is by Mr. *Collier* opened to every Body, she is asham'd of the Pleasure her Hypocrisie can no longer protect her in. These
are the unavoidable Complements Mr. *Collier* makes the
Ladies of Vertue and Honour, as well as Quality, who
ever have, and still do, frequent the Theatre.

Dor. No wonder he shou'd tell us of his Surprize that
Vertue had yet any footing among us, when this was
his Notion of the Finest, most Sensible, and most Vertuous, Women of the World.

Ura. This is his engaging Way to draw our Admiration of his Book——— But, Ladies and Gentlemen,
the Evening is warm, and the Moon shines so bright,
that I fancy a Walk in the Garden will not be ungrate-
ful, and the cool Breeze of the Wind may qualifie the
heat of your Dispute.

Lord Vaunt. Refuse me, Medem, I think your Ladiship
admirably in the right of it. [*Aside.*] So I may get an
Opportunity of Straggling with *Eliza* from the rest of the
Company,

Company, and make thofe Advances a *Cavalier*, fo well vers'd in Gallantry, ought to do to a Lady alone.

Dor. 'Twill be at leaft an agreeable Ceffation for us to recover Breath, and our Adverfaries their Temper; we'll therefore wait on your Lordfhip.

> *For Paffion never will to Juftice yield;*
> *Tho' vanquifh'd, ftill pretends to keep the Field;*
> *Will make a boaft of empty Trophies won,*
> *And with falfe Heat their known Difgrace difown.*

The End of the Second Act.

ACT III. SCENE, *A Garden.*

Enter Sir Jerry Witwoud *and* Dorimant.

Dor. THus you fee, Sir *Jerry,* that I have made out
that the Stage is the School of Vertue, where
Vice and Folly are expos'd, and Vertue promoted; or
to put it into Mr. *Collier's* own Words, which are more
prevalent with you, I have made it appear that the Bufinefs of the Stage is to Recommend Vertue, and Difcountenance Vice, to fhew the Uncertainty of Humane Greatnefs, the fudden Turns of Fate, and the unhappy Conclufions of Violence and Injuftice, to expofe the Singularity of Pride and Fancy, to make Folly and Falfhood
Contemptible, and to bring every thing that is ill under
Infamy and Negleƈt.

Sir Jerry. Go on, Sir———

Dor. Now, Sir *Jerry,* from this Maxim of Mr. *Collier's,*
it follows that thefe Vices, and thefe Follies, muft be
drawn, or elfe they cou'd not be expos'd. Is it not therefore an Argument of an Inveterate Hypocrite that makes
your Reformers fuch Enemies to the Stage? If you are
fuch Zealots for Morality, firft Reform your felves———
Next, pray why are you lefs fevere on Taverns, Brandy-
Shops, and other Tippling-houfes, on Gaming-Tables,

H   Ufurers,

Ufurers, Oppreffors of the Poor, Betrayers of the Publick, Libellers of the State and Church, and the like.

Sir Jerry. We muft do all things by degrees.

Dor. You begin therefore with your Endeavours to fupprefs that which from your own Confeffion is ufeful to the promoting the End you pretend to, and let thofe things alone to hereafter which all the World with one Voice condemn as pernicious to Vertue and to Mankind. And let me tell you, Sir *Jerry*, if the Stage did not make its Bufinefs to expofe Knaves and Hypocrites, you wou'd fay nothing to it; 'tis becaufe it declares againft you that you are fo Clamorous againft that.

Sir Jerry. Well, well, Mr. *Dorimant*, let all Mankind, Reafon and Demonftration, fay what they will, I'm fure I'm in the right——

Dor. There indeed fpoke the Enemies of the Stage all in one; you are a Pleafant Arguer, Sir *Jerry*, on my Word.

Sir Jerry. But you have not touch'd one thing, the meeting of fo many lewd People together.

Dor. The fame meet at the Church, the Meeting-houfe, the *Park*, *Epfom*, *Tunbridge*, &c.

Sir Jerry. All, all unlawful Meetings, where there are above Two or Three.

Dor. Ha! ha! ha! But fee the Ladies——

Enter Lord Vaunt-Title, Urania, Eliza, *and* Clemene.

Eliz. My Lord, I proteft I can gather nothing from all you have faid but the very great Efteem you have for your own Quality.

Lord Vaunt. And don't you think, Medem, that others ought to have the like, refufe me! Ha!

Eliz. Refufe you I fhall for all that I can difcover in your Lordfhip——

Clem.

Clem. Eh! Ged, Medem, you deſtroy my Night's Reſt by one word more for the Stage; it has loſt me all the Pleaſure of this Moon-light Walk about your Charming Gardens—— Oh, Sir *Jerry,* I'm ſure I come to join in your Triumph over this obſtinate One.

Dor. Faith, Madam, we have been like true Diſputants, both weary, but neither convinc'd. But I have made a conſiderable Diſcovery, Madam *Clemene,* which will ſhock your eſteem for Sir *Jerry.*

Ura. Ah! Pray let us hear that, Mr. *Dorimant,* for that wou'd be Triumph indeed.

Clem. But a Triumph, Medem, that your Ladiſhip, let me dey, will not obtein.

Dor. I can aſſure you that he is now going on a Work that will for ever diſoblige you.

Clem, Eh! Ged, Mr. *Dorimant,* that's impoſſible!

Dor. Nay, I confeſs I may be deceiv'd, and you that cou'd ſacrifice your Reaſon to his Opinion, may, perhaps, diſcharge your Pleaſure and Inclination too on that Account.

Clem. That you may be ſure of, Mr. *Dorimant,* for, Gad forgive me, I was too too wickedly inclin'd to ſee thoſe filthy Plays, 'til he and Mr. *Collier* made me a Convert——

Dor. Hear then, Madam, thus it is—— having depriv'd you of all Rational and Honourable Recreations, he proceeds to confound your meer Diverſions too, as *Tunbridge, Epſom,* the *Bath, Richmond, Lambeth,* and *Iſlington, Wells, High-Park,* the *Mall, Spring-Garden,* nay, the very Fields that lead to thoſe wicked Places, are to go down; Vice and Vanity are to be diſpatch'd Root and Branch, and you muſt, (as a *French Popiſh* Prelate has it) like the Innocent *Jews,* divert your ſelves with your Children at home.

Ura. But what if we have none?

Lord Vaunt. Rat me, Medem, you muſt get 'em, he! he! he! Refuſe me if *Dorimant* be not a pleaſant Fellow, ha! ha! ha!

Clem.

Clem. Eh! Good Mr. *Dorimant*, you kill me———— you suffocate me; you put me into infupportable Convulfions!———— No *Epfom!* No *Tunbridge!* Impoffible! It cannot be! Speak, Sir *Jerry*———— Are you fo furioufly Cruel to take away from the Ladies our beloved *Tunbridge*, and all that?

Sir Jerry. Moft certainly, Madam; the Work of Godlinefs is not to be done by halves! What avails the fhutting the Doors of that Houfe of *Dagon*, the Play-houfe, if we leave him the Hills and High Places? To drive the Devil from his Chamber-Practice, and leave him the Fields?

Clem. Eh! Ged! But the poor People, let me dey, 'twill be hard on the Inhabitants of thofe Places, Sir *Jerry*, who live by the Refort of Company.

Sir Jerry. So do the debauch'd Actors, Madam———— but for the future let Godlinefs be a Gain, and let the Wicked Starve! For Wealth gives Confideration! Now I'm for making People rich by Vertue, and fo turn the Pomp and Vanity of the World to the better fide. If People got Eftates by Religion, how wou'd the Churches be throng'd, and the Clergy ador'd? For Wealth gives Confideration———— I ftick to that———— 'Tis true, 'tis hard for the People of *Epfom*, *Tunbridge*, &c. to Starve———— yet the Herb of the Field, and the Water of the Brook, will prevent that———— The Patriarchs fed fo, and why not they? If they wou'd fare better, let 'em come into our Reforming Project.

Clem. But let me dey, Sir *Jerry*, this is furioufly extravagant———— Perfons of all Sorts go thither to drink the Waters for the Cure of Diftempers, and the like, Sir *Jerry*.

Sir Jerry. Ay, ay, Madam———— and the like may fignifie much; but as for the reft, they are meer Pretences to get Opportunities of Wickednefs, for can't they have the Waters brought home? Is it decent, do you think, to have fo many Men and Women meet together? Is not the Devil ready enough at home, but they muft go feek him out, and

and run into Temptations— The Ancient *Pagans* were more cautious ; their Young Maids, nay, and their Matrons too, were never permitted to go abroad to Publick Meetings, and were only treated by their Relations ; and ev'n in this wicked Age, all *Italy, Spain, Portugal, Greece, Natolia,* in ſhort, all *Aſia* and *Africa,* manage them ſo ſtill.

Dor. Right, Sir *Jerry,* I am now your Convert, there is a Majority againſt the Practice of our Ladies ; and the Rules of Modeſty muſt be taken from the greater number ; for ſo Mr. *Collier* does for the Stage, and the Stage is the Image of the World.

Sir Jerry. Well, I can't forbear ſaying an honeſt *Heathen* or *Turk* is none of the worſt *Chriſtians* ; and a very indifferent Religion well believ'd will go a great way.

Dor. I ſubmit, Sir *Jerry,* I Swear you have Conquer'd ; You have Ten *Colliers* in your Belly ; for this is infinitely more to the Purpoſe than all he has urg'd.

Sir Jerry. Do you think that it is not highly Immodeſt for Men and Women to meet at the *Wells,* and drink the ſame Waters ? But then is it not Monſtrous, moſt *Babyloniſh,* and Obſcene, for Men and Women to go into the *Bath* together ? Do you not imagine on thoſe Occaſions the Men have Paſſions rais'd that cannot be diſcharg'd without Trouble, or ſatisfied without a Crime, as Mr. *Collier* ſays——

Dor. Admirable, Sir *Jerry,* he ſpeaks like an Oracle.

Sir Jerry. Is not the Tranſition eaſie from one Sex to another ? As thus at the *Wells*——the Waters are the ſame, they paſs the ſame way, and the diſtance that parts 'em is too ſmall to keep off the Imagination which is Pregnant on theſe Occaſions— Filthy Idea's will preſent themſelves before us— and the whole Scene of *Smut*— to ſay no worſe— will come in view—

Dor. Excellent, Sir *Jerry.*

Sir Jerry. As for Example, the Gallant drinks the Water with his Miſtreſs (I mean his Whore) for I'm for giving every

ry

ry thing its proper Name; to complement Vice, is next
Door to worſhipping the Devil; they both take their turns,
having firſt wiſhed each other's Water a free Paſſage; (Oh the
Lewdneſs of the Age) it begins to work with him, this puts
him in mind of what it may do with her; this leads his
Mind down the Ladies Walk, (I cry you Mercy, down the
Whores Walk) while Neceſſity forces his Body down the
Mens——

Ura. But why don't you call the Mens Walk the Rogues,
Sir *Jerry?*

Sir Jerry. No Interrupting—— Well, he arrives at the Place
of Eaſe, that puts him in mind whereabouts ſhe is, and
when 'tis come to that Women do not——

Clem. Eh! Ged, let me dey, Sir *Jerry*, you are furiouſly
Impertinent——

All. Ha! ha! ha! ha! ha!

Sir Jerry. Nay, Madam, I ſhall not Complement Vice, 'tis but
one Remove from worſhipping the Devil. I muſt go on——

Clem. For Heav'ns ſake, Sir, conſider where you are,
and among whom—— Modeſty is the Character of our Sex;
and Men that entertain Women with rude Diſcourſe affront
them; (as Mr. *Collier* ſays) to Treat Ladies with ſuch Stuff,
is to preſume on their Patience to abuſe them.

Sir Jerry. Ay, ay, Madam, you may ſay what you pleaſe,
but I ſhall go on—— Humility is a Vertue, but Meanneſs and
ſneaking Civility to Vice is below my Character—— I muſt go
on, Madam——

Ura.
Eliz. } And we'll go off then.

Ura. If theſe be your Stage Reformers, deliver us from
their Doctrine by a ſpeedy conveyance of them to *Bedlam*——
[*Exeunt Ura. Eliz.*

Lord Vaunt. Ha! My Pert *Eliza* ſlipt away! I'll after her.
[*Exit.*

Clem. I vow you have frighten'd away Madam *Urania* and
her

her Cousin ; but, Sir *Jerry,* won't you allow the *Bath ?* You know the Quality goes there.

Sir Jerry. I am no respecter of Persons, the *Bath* is the worst of all, for that is like putting Men and Women to Bed together : *O Tempora ! O Mores !*

Clem. Will you not then allow Men and Women to meet——

Sir Jerry. No, marry won't I——What shou'd they meet for ? What uses to follow the meeting of Man and Woman ? Wickedness, wickedness ; are we not forbid to look on a Woman ? And can Women appear in Publick without Dressing, and showing their Faces ? Nay, their naked Necks and Breasts ! And then you know how easie the Transition is from one Part of the naked Body to the other ; the Devil is always at hand, and the Flesh always about us—— The Eyes, the Nose, the Mouth, and every Part, in short, of a Pretty Woman administers lewd Thoughts. If she have a pretty little Mouth—— why presently Men are drawing lewd Consequences ; by a fine Hand and Arm, they will be led to a handsom Leg and Foot, and thence the Bars are too feeble to hinder more Criminal Approaches—— And what need is there of all this ? Have Men enter'd into a League with Wicked-ness, and are they not content with the Ills of Solitude, but they must hunt after more in Company ? Believe me, Madam, I know it by Experience, all Mankind are deprav'd in their Appetites and Inclinations, and Vice (as Mr. *Collier* proves) is more inviting than Vertue—— Man was made in Solitude—— Society was the Invention of Luxury ; and he that built the first City was a Murderer—— When in the Woods the Noble Savage ran—— then there was no Whoring, no Immorality and Prophaneness ; no Whoring, Madam—— every Man kept his Wife or Concubine to himself—— there was no *Epsom,* no *Tunbridge,* no *Bath,* no *Richmond,* and the like, to draw Whores and Rogues together—— Nay, these Places are worse than the Play-houses, for there is nothing else to divert
them

them from corrupting Mens Wives, and spending their Money, from Gaming, Drinking, and all that— but at the Play, the wicked Play it self may engage them awhile— Then at these Places Opportunity gives both Temptation and Relief; at the Play-house some Accident may hinder, or at least defer, their Wickedness.

Dor. Ten to One, Sir *Jerry*, but that's the Reason the Ladies have so forsaken the *Theatre*.

Clem. Eh! Gad, Sir *Jerry*, no more, you have furiously mov'd my Aversion, let me dey.

Sir Jerry. Why, Madam? Do not the City spend their Estates at these lewd Places? Are not they the Market of Sharpers? The Expence of Plays is a Trifle to them, Madam: Besides, the City Wives meet their Gallants there, and abuse their poor Husbands with the greater ease, by the promiscuous Meeting of all Company there, and the abominable Liberty of the Place.

Dor. Nay, I'll ev'n withdraw, for I know not when he'll ha' done, as long as he has any Hearers of an Adverse Party.
                                                                    [*Exit.*

Sir Jerry. Nay, as if Dressing, Ogling, and so forth, wou'd not do it. They Dance together in Publick too, which heats their Blood, that stirs up their Imagination, that sets fire to their Desires, and that blows up their Vertue, and makes 'em run mad to make use of Opportunity; for their Motion and Action have a strange Force on the Inclinations: They add to the Charms of the Person that were too strong before, and deprive us of all that shou'd make our Defence. [*Looking about*] I protest, Madam, we are left alone!— And now, Madam, I cannot lose this Opportunity of paying my grateful Acknowledgment to your Ladiship for Espousing my Cause; for were it not for those frail Ladies that we have made Converts, I protest the Poets wou'd run us down. But these Ladies being great Coquets, engage the Beaux that pretend to Wit, and such a Party will gain any Cause.

                                                                    Clem.

Clem. But you have loft your Caufe with me, let me dey! If you go on at this rate— you have fo furioufly provok'd me I cou'd almoft have found in my Heart to have difcover'd you to be a Falfe Brother in a Lay Habit. But pray, by the Way, why have you left off your Gown?

Sir Jerry. Becaufe fome Accidents may happen, Madam, that may bring a Scandal on the Gown; and now whatever I fay or do falls on the Prophane Laity, and fo I give Sir *John Brute* a *Rowland* for his *Oliver.*

Clem. But, Sir *Jerry,* you that correct us all need not fear that; you can be in no danger of bringing Scandal, who bring fo much Glory to the Gown.

Sir Jerry. —Alas! Madam, we are all Mortal—all Flefh is frail. And do you think, Madam, that any Man alive cou'd fay fo many fevere things on both Sexes, without having had a fufficient Experience of thofe Evils and Frailties in himfelf?— And Gratitude, join'd with thefe Tranfcendent Charms, which your Ladifhip difplays in your Refplendent Face, are fo Tranfporting, and fo Enthufiaftick, that I am borne out of my felf, and abfolutely forc'd on what I can't avoid— Oh! Madam, you have rais'd a Paffion that cannot be difcharg'd without trouble.

Clem. What?; Nor fatisfy'd without a Crime.

Sir Jerry. That I don't know— What is a Crime to the Wicked, may not be fo to the Godly. If you guard well the Appearance, half the Duty of Religion is preferv'd, and you avoid the Scandal; now the Crime, as to Men, is not none, if not known; and in many reputed Crimes the Scandal is all the Offence: Remove that, and the Crime vanifhes; as particularly in a Private Amour, where there is no Injury—

Clem. Eh! let me dey, if this be not furioufly furprifing——

Sir Jerry. Or if it were a Crime, you look fo killing Fair, you juftifie Rebellion— And I can no longer wafte Words

I   where

where Opportunity is so fair. Modesty is the Character of your Sex, and Boldness of mine— Now Boldness requires Action, and Modesty Passion— that is, I must attaque you, and you must not resist— and so the *Decorum* and *Character* of both Sexes are preserv'd. If the Poets wou'd bring their Lovers to Action without so many Words, 'twere something— but their fine Women often lose their Reputation by their Coqueting, and might cheaper be happy in Deed than in Talk— They seem fond of the Scandal, and fearful of the Pleasure; whereas the Pleasure shou'd engage their Fondness, and the Scandal their Fear.

Clem. Admirable Doctrine, let me dey.

Sir Jerry. Are you pleas'd with it, Madam?— Let me dey, (for I will not swear as much as by those bright Eyes, or those pretty Lips) if I will not immediately reduce it to Practice—— for till then it is but a useless Speculation.

[*Offers to kiss and embrace it.*

Clem. Let me dey, if you are not furiously Rude, Sir *Jerry*— Oh! Sir, Pray, pray— Eged— What, will you attempt upon my Honour?

Sir Jerry. Not on your Honour, Madam, only on your Person—— your Honour is only in Words, but your Pleasure in Deeds. Come, come, we are alone, I all over Love, and you all over Charms!

Clem. Eh! Lard! Sir *Jerry*, I swear I'll run away from you.

Sir Jerry. Come, come, you must not strive any longer against your own Satisfaction—— your Honour's safe—— put, put off the Veil, I know you're a Hypocrite.

Clem. Nay, now you begin to be Abusive, I vow I'll call out if you won't let me alone——— A Hypocrite?

Sir Jerry. Nay, I'm sure of it, for almost all our Party are so.

Clem. Eh! Let me dey, if you be not furiously Abusive— and yet let me dey again, he is a Charming Person— he has
Wit,

Wit, nay, and Difcretion too— and 'tis his Intereft befides to keep all Secret; he knows I find that I am a Hypocrite, and what if I confirm him mine by letting him into the Secret, 'twill engage him to Celebrate me as a Vertuous Patronefs of his Works— Eh! Fee, Sir *Jerry,* I'll call out— Eh! Ged, what are you doing— Sir *Jerry*— I fwear we fhall be caught, let me dey!

Sir Jerry. Ay, ay, with Pleafure, Madam; Gad, if I don't give the Formal Ladies fome Encouragement this Way, our Caufe will fall— Oh! my Life! my Soul! my——

Enter the Company Laughing.

All. Ha! ha! ha! he! he! he! he!

Dor. Why, how now, Sir *Jerry!* What, a Rape? Blefs us, What's become of our *Anti-Epfomift?* What, is this the Effect of Solitude?

Ura. What, in my Garden too? Oh! hideous— Sir *Jerry,* I owe fomething to your *Quondam* Gown (for we have heard all) or my Footmen and Horfe-pond fhou'd revenge the Affront.

Dor. But my Lady *Clemene*— What, will you ever go to the Wicked, Debauch'd, Lewd, Play-houfe any more, when the Confounder of the Stage can fo much better divert you?

Clem. Let me dey, my Lady *Urania,* I'm overjoy'd that you came to my Refcue— for let me dey, what is a weak Woman in fuch a Man's Hands— But let me dey, if Sir *Jerry* be not a Perfon that of all Perfons I never took for fuch a Perfon; but he is become furioufly my Averfion, and in revenge I will go every Day this Week to the Play-houfe—

Sir Jerry. Gentlemen, I am caught——but I hope, fince my Zeal has been private here, fo you'll let my Folly be. For if the damn'd Poets fhou'd get this Story by the end, I fhall be Worried to Death by 'em; I afk your Pardon, Lady, and fo good Night.

Ura. But'tis fit such a Hypocrite fhou'd be expos'd.

Sir Jerry. Ah! No—— if the Hypocrites were expos'd, half the Town wou'd go naked—— and all the Stage Enemies, like me, go off with their Tails betwixt their Legs.

[*Exit.*

Dor. Well, whatever Grave Pretences fome may make,
'Tis for a Truth, let all that hear me take,
Thofe that with Singular and Peculiar Pride,
Set up for Vertue above all befide,
Do but with cunning Art great Faults difguife,
And fteal their guilty Joys from our obferving Eyes;
At harmlefs Pleafures they with fury rail,
That they the better may their Blots conceal.

F I N I S.

ADVERTISEMENT.

The Author being out of Town when thefe Sheets were Printed off, the Reader is defir'd before he perufe the Book to correct with his Pen the following *Errata.*

Page 2. line 39. for *then* read *therefore,* l. 40. dele *for,* p. 3. l. 20. after *when* add *Vertue,* and for *Vice* r. *Difh,* l. 22. after *Vertue* only a Comma, l. 25. for on r. or, l. 39. after *will* add *be.* p. 4. l. 13. for *Vice* r. *Voice,* l. 19. after *Reputation* add *and,* p. 5. l. 16. after *Folly* add *to,* l. 27. for *Reverence* r. *Revenue,* l. 29. in the place of the Dafh add *Wound,* l. 32. after *me* add *felf,* and l 42. for *leaft* r. *laft.* p. 6. l. 30. for *not* r. *nor,* l. 41. for *be* r. *fay,* p. 8. l. 31. for *a* r. *the,* l. 34. in the Space put *touz'd,* p. 9. l. 2. for *Parts* r. *Poets,* l. 20. in the Space put *Epithets,* l. 24. for *Belly Paffi:n* r. *Belle-Paffion,* l. 30. for *its* r. *as,* p. 11. l. 3. for *Pulpit* r. *Culprit,* p. 13. l. 1. for *Spiritual* r. *Spirituelle,* l. 2. after *Matter* add *to convince,* l. 25. for *Ambign* r. *Ambigue,* for *Word* r. *uaid,* l. *penult.* for *Confiruffion* r. *Opinion,* p. 23. l. 31. for *fame* r. *Scene.* There are feveral litteral Faults which are left to the Reader.

A N

AN
EPILOGUE,
UPON THE
Reformers;
SPOKEN BY
Mr. *WILKS*, at the *Theatre-Royal in Drury-lane.*

WELL, *Gentlemen, this boldly we may say,*
    Howe'er you like it, 'tis a Modest Play;
There's no Prophaneness, and no Bawdy, in't;
No, not one single double-meaning hint;
And that's enough in so Reform'd an Age,
For all our Author to reform the Stage.
'Tis now some Years since Drowsie Reformation
Rous'd its dull Head, and saw its Restoration
What Influence has this had upon the Nation?

Ye

The Epilogue.

Ye Rakehells of the Rose, let Rouse confess
If at his House he draws one Hogshead less.
And you intriguing Sparks enquire of Jenny
If it has baulk'd her of one Bawdy Guinea.
Is Gaming grown a less destructive Vice?
Are fewer Families undone by Dice?
No— for the Cunning Men the Town infest,
And daily for new Quarries are in quest.
Oft times in Publick they their Ends arrive at,
But Shoals of Bubbles are drawn in in private.
'Tis by these Means they furnish out Debauches,
And Sharpers now like Quacks set up their Coaches.
Now let us cast our Eyes upon the City,
These are no Vices— no— none that are Witty.
Expensive are the sprightly Sins of Wits,
But frugal, gainful, Vices are for Cits.
They never Swear, because for that they Pay,
But they will Lie— yet— in a Trading Way.
They've Lies in readiness whene'er they Barter,
And claim the Right of Cheating from their Charter.
They with Suburbian Whores ne'er lead their Lives,
But why?— why, they can't satisfie their Wives.
Besides, with Cost the Suburb Punk they Treat,
But they will drink, because e'en drunk they Cheat.
Examine all the Town, each Quarter view,
And we shall find what Butler said is true,
We all are proud for Sins we are inclin'd to,
By damning those we never have a mind to.
Thus Reformation has discharg'd its Rage
Upon the Vices of the Sinking Stage.
As Ships
When fraught with Foreign Luxury they sail,
As soon as ever they descry a Whale
Throw out a Tub to find the Monster play,
Lest the rich Cargo shou'd become its Prey.

The Epilogue.

So some to turn our furious Zealot's Rage
From lov'd high Crimes have overthrown the Stage.
Gentlemen, briefly this has been our Fault,
We more for others than our selves have Thought.
Each Man wou'd piously reform his Neighbour;
To save himself he thinks not worth his Labour.
With Zeal and Sin at once we're strangely warm'd,
And grow more Wicked as we grow Reform'd.
Oh! 'tis a blessed Age, and blessed Nation,
When Vice walks cheek by jowl with Reformation.
In short, let each Man's Thoughts first look at home,
And then to Foreign Reformations roam.
If all the Fools and Knaves met here to Day,
Wou'd their own Faults and Follies first Survey,
We need not fear their Censures of the Play.

F I N I S.

BOOKS newly Printed, and Sold by John Nutt, near Stationers-Hall.

THE Miscellaneous Works written by his Grace *George* late Duke of *Buckingham*, containing Poems, Satyrs, Letters, and his Speeches in Parliament; with a Collection of Speeches by several Noble Peers and Commoners in the Three last Reigns. Price 5 *s.*

The *Source* of our *Present Fears* discover'd: Or, Plain Proof of some late Designs against our *Present Constitution* and *Government:* Containing *Remarks* on *Scandalous Libels* and *Pamphlets* published of late, and a Justification of some Passages in a late Book, Intituled, *The History of the last Sessions of Parliament,* written by the *Author of the last Parliament.* Price 1 *s.*

Familiar.

Familiar and Courtly Letters, in Three Parts, in One Volume, written to several Persons of Honour and Quality. By Monf. *Voiture*, a Member of the Royal Academy of *Paris* ; made English by Mr. *Dreyden*, *Tho. Cheek*, Efq; Mr. *Dennis*, *Hen. Cromwel*, Efq; Mr. *Ralphfon*, Fellow of the Royal Society ; Dr.— &c. with Select. Epiftles out of *Ariftænetus*, Tranflated from the Greek : Some Select Letters out of *Pliny*, Junior, and *M. Fontenelle*; and a Collection of Original Letters lately written on feveral Subjects, and now much improv'd. By Mr. *T. Brown*. To which is added, A Collection of Letters of Friendfhip, and other Occafional Letters, written by Mr. *Dreyden*, Mr. *Wycherly*, Mr.—— Mr. *Congreve*, and Mr. *Dennis*. The Third Edition with large Additions. Price 4 *s*.

An Effay on Ways and Means to maintain the Honour and Safety of *England*, to encreafe Trade, Merchandize, Navigation, Shipping, Mariners and Sea-men, in War and Peace. Written by Sir *Walter Raleigh*, Kt. With ufeful Remarks and Obfervations towards the Improvement of our Habours, Ports, and Havens. By Sir *Henry Sheers*, Kt. Price 6 *d*.

A General and Comical View of the Cities of *London* and *Weftminfter*: Or, Mr. *Sylvefter Partridge*'s Infallible Predictions ; in Two Parts : Giving an Impartial Account of feveral Merry Humours, Occurrences and Intrigues, that will be transacted amongft all Degrees of People, and in all manner of Places, down from the Beau to the Bellows-mender ; and the Nice *Eaft-India* Lady to the *Covent-Garden* Crack ; and from *Weftminfter Hall* to the *Bear-Garden*, for thefe Six Months *October*, *November*, *December*, *January*, *February*, and *March*. Price 1 *s*.

The Secret Hiftory of the *Calves-Head Club* : Or, The *Republican* Unmask'd ; wherein is fully fhewn the Religion of the *Calves-Head Heroes*, in their Anniverfary Thankfgiving Songs on the Thirtieth of *January*, by them called *Anthems*, for the Years 1693, 1694, 1695, 1696, 1697. Now Publifhed to demonftrate the Reftlefs, Implacable, Spirit of a certain Party ftill among us, who are never to be fatisfied till the prefent Eftablifhment in Church and State as fubverted. The Fourth Edition with Additions, Corrected. Dedicated to the Obfervator.

A FARTHER

VINDICATION

OF THE

SHORT VIEW

OF THE

PROFANENESS

AND

IMMORALITY

OF THE

𝕰𝔫𝔤𝔩𝔦𝔰𝔥 𝔖𝔱𝔞𝔤𝔢,

In which the

OBJECTIONS

Of a late Book, Entituled,

A Defence of Plays,

ARE CONSIDER'D.

By *JEREMY COLLIER,* M. A.

LONDON:
Printed for *R. Sare* at *Gray's-Inn-Gate* in *Holborn,* and
G. Strahan at the *Golden Ball* in *Cornhill.* 1708.

A
REPLY
TO
Dr. *FILMER*'s
DEFENCE of PLAYS, &c.

HAVING receiv'd no Anſwer to
my *Second Defence* [a] of my *Short
View*, &c. in ſeven Years, I con-
cluded the *Stage-Controverſie* was
over. But there's no reckoning upon the In-
termiſſions of a Conteſt. Dr. *Filmer* has at
laſt enter'd the Liſts, and reviv'd the Quarrel. It muſt be ſaid this Gentleman has given himſelf time enough to make his Attack, and bring up the Forces of the Cauſe.
The Supplies of Converſation, the Remarks
of the Criticks, and all the Succours of the
Play-Houſe Confederacy muſt probably have

[a] *A Reply to
the Ancient
and Modern
Stages ſur-
vey'd, &c.*

reach'd

reach'd him before now. By taking *Horace's* Advice, of

⁺ De Arte
Poet.

—*Nonumq; premantur in annum,* ᵇ

He has had great leifure for bringing his Thoughts to Review and Recollection. But then as fome things improve, fo others decay upon Time. Now whether the Doctor is a Sufferer this way or not ; whether his Hand has not fhook, and his Aim been broken by levelling thus long, the *Reader* muft judge.

Before I come to debate the Difference between us, I muft acquaint the *Reader,* how far we are agreed : And here the Doctor goes a great length in his Conceffions. He owns the *Stage* guilty of remarkable *Abufes.* That this Mifbehaviour has *made a great Noife in the World* ᶜ; *that a due regulation in thefe Matters has been expected, and earneftly defir'd by the moft fober part of the Nation* ᵈ : *That many of our Modern Poets have been very much to blame, and err'd in Fundamentals. They feem,* fays this Gentleman, *to have made choice of Characters only for their Lewdnefs, and have frequently crown'd Vice with the Reward of Virtue* ᵉ. He confeffes, the *Comick Poets have mifmanag'd to a horrible Excefs of Libertinifm and Irreligion :* And that the *Tragedies*

ᶜ Dr. Filmer's Defence of
Plays.Pref.
p. 1, 2.
ᵈ Pref. p.4.

ᵉ Id. Book
p. 4.

(5)

gedies produc'd in the View, *&c. are irregular in the distribution of Rewards and Punishments* [f]. In short, he makes no difficulty to say, the Disorders of the *Stage* have given me a very fair opportunity of exposing our Poets as Atheists, and representing *the Stage as a place hated by God, and haunted by the Devil* [g].

In discoursing upon the Head of Profaneness, he grants *many of the Quotations cited by me, are extremely scandalous and wicked* [h]. He is positive, *nothing either Atheistical or Irreligious; nothing in the least Profane, should fall from under the Comick Poet's Pen, under any pretence of Character whatsoever* [i]. He honestly declares, *no Story, no Phrase, no Expression whatsoever in the* Bible, *may be repeated, or so much as alluded to, without Sin* [k]. And though he is now abridging the Liberties of *Comedy*, yet the compass of his Assertion, and the Force of his Reasoning, affects *Tragedy*, and reaches the *Stage*, under all distinctions. And here he goes on, declaiming against the abuse of *Scripture*, with a strong Air of Conscience, and fair Meaning.

After all this acknowledgment, and more to the same purpose, who could have expected a *Play-House* Advocate in the Doctor? On the other hand, since the Liberties continue unreform'd; since they *Act* their foul

A 3   *detected*

detected *Plays* over again; since their *new* Plays are [1] short of the Doctor's Reformation; since the Case stands thus, one would have thought he should rather have exerted himself against the incorrigibleness of the *Theatre*, and endeavour'd to dissuade the *Town* from frequenting so infectious a Place, so scandalous a Diversion. One would have thought he might have propos'd at least some new Remedy, mov'd for some significant *Test*, and suggested the seizure of counterband Goods: That he would have erected an *Office* of *Reformation*, a Court of Justice, where the Judge might not be prepossess'd in favour of the Criminal, nor the *Bench*, and the *Bar* hold Intelligence with each other. His pleading for the *Play-House*, while it continues in *Face Romuli*, and goes on in the old Road, argues, either that he does not perceive the consequence of his Concessions, (which excuse can hardly be made for a Man of the Doctor's Understanding) or else, that all his Pretences for *Reformation*, are nothing but Amusement and Grimace. Indeed I wish there is not more of Art than good Earnest, in the Doctor's Scheme. By this expectation, that *Matters will mend*, the present Disorders are more under Cover, and the Mischief has the freer Passage. And thus, if we will but swallow Poyson

[1] *Recruiting Officer. Tunbridge-Walks, &c.*

a

a little while, we fhall be fed with better Diet afterwards.

And yet after all, we fhall find the Doctor's *Noftrum's* are much too weak to reach the Difeafe, and carry off the ill Humours. To fpeak clearly, he confiders the *Palate* too much in his *Bill*, and prefcribes more to Pleafure than Health.

Having premis'd the Doctor's *canceffions*, I fhall proceed to joyn Iffue with him, and engage the force of his *Book.*

To fhew the Stage was not left to the Liberties of *Heathen* precedents, I cited St. *Paul* for my Authority. His words are thefe. *But Fornication, and all Uncleannefs, or Covetoufnefs, let it not be once named among you, as becometh Saints. Neither Filthinefs, nor foolifh Talking, nor Jefting, which are not convenient* [m]. The Doctor, to avoid the Rebuke of this plain Text, endeavours to turn part of it upon me. He pretends, if thefe words are to be taken in a literal Senfe, then *Covetoufnefs* muft not be nam'd any more than the reft : *And yet I have given up this Vice to the Stage Poets, to make Sport with* [n].

To this I need only obferve, that Πλεονεξία, which is tranflated *Covetoufnefs*, imports unnatural Debauchery, and comes up to the Sin for which *Sodom* and *Gomorrah* were deftroy'd. Thus the learned Dr. *Hammond*

[m] *Ephef. v.* 3, 4.

[n] *Firft Defence of the Short View, &c.* P. 8.

[n] *Dr. Filmer's Defence of Plays*, p. 18, 19.

mond underſtands the Original, and proves his Interpretation from the Connexion of the *words*, from other places in the *Old* and *New Teſtament*, and from the common uſe of it in this Senſe, among Pagan Authors [o].

[o] Hammon. in Loc. & Annot. on Rom. i.

Dr. *Filmer* goes on with the *Text*, and ſeems very much diſturb'd at the rigour of the *Precept. I never knew before*, ſays he, *that a Chriſtian could not break a Jeſt*, *without breaking a Commandment* [p].

[p] Dr. Filmer. p. 20.

To relieve him a little, he may pleaſe to take notice, that *jeſting* is joyn'd by the Apoſtle with *fooliſh talking*. Now that Μωρολογια, or *fooliſh talking*, ſignifies rank, luſcious, and ſcandalous Converſation; the Learned *Hammond* makes out to a full Evidence. And thus the *jeſting* condemn'd by the Apoſtle, imports ſmutty Diſcourſe made uſe of for Laughing and Diverſion. And that the *Heathens* look'd upon theſe as unwarrantable Latitudes, I have prov'd from the Teſtimonies of *Euripides, Ariſtotle*, and *Livy* [q].

[*] Ibid. in Loc.

[q] View, &c. p. 35, 159, 160, 161.

The Doctor perceiving the *Stage* lie terribly expos'd, enters his Caveat, and tells us, *This is ſtretching our Apoſtle's meaning to a higher pitch than ever he intended* [r]. How does this appear ? Becauſe, as he argues, when St. *Paul* recapitulates theſe Crimes in the fifth Verſe, he repeats *Fornication*, and *Uncleanneſs*, &c. *but not a word*

[r] Defence of Plays, p. 21.

word of obscene and filthy Talking [*Ibid.*]. Does
the Doctor infer an allowance from this
Omiſſion ? Becauſe the Apoſtle does not go
the whole length in his Repetition, therefore he has given a toleration for Smut and
Indecency ! Is not one plain Prohibition
ſtrong enough to bind the Conſcience ?
Are we not to take notice of the Divine
Laws, unleſs they are repeated upon us ?
However, if this ungodly Liberty would
paſs, the Doctor is in no condition to claim
the Benefit. For the Precept in queſtion,
is frequently inculcated by the ſame Apoſtle. The places are theſe. *Evil Commu-* [1 Cor. xv.
nication corrupts good Manners. Let no cor- 33.
rupt Communication proceed out of your Epheſ. iv.
Mouth. But now you put off all filthy Com- 29.
munication. I am ſorry I have an Adver- Coloſ. iii.
ſary that makes this Quotation neceſſary. 8.]
The Confidence of ſome Men ! For here I
can't forbear uſing the Doctor's civil Ex-
clamation. But I muſt take notice of his
other Evaſion. He gives me to underſtand,
that unleſs I *can make out, the Apoſtle for-*
bids all obſcene filthy Talking and Jeſting,
under the ſame Penalty that he does Forni-
cation, and actual Uncleanneſs, he can't ſee
the Text above cited can do half the intend-
ed Execution [*Defence of*
. Not forbidden under the *Plays. ibid.*]
ſame Penalties ! They are plainly con-
demned as unlawful Liberties. They are
forbidden

forbidden as Heathen Impurities, and a
breach of the Engagements of Baptism; as
inconsistent with the Sobriety of Christians, and the Dignity of Saints. The ven-
turing therefore upon this Practice, must
of necessity incur the Divine Displeasure,
forfeit our future Happiness; and then
the Doctor knows what must follow. What
though foul Talking is not so bad as Fornication? A Man may be lost without going to the highest degrees of Guilt. Steal-
ing is not so bad as Murther; and yet
Thieves, without Repentance, *shall not in-*
berit the Kingdom of God.

I Cor. vi. 10.

The Doctor, rather than part with the
Stage Entertainment, is so hardy as to affirm, that *Filthiness, and foolish Talking,*
are censur'd no farther in the Text, than
as inconvenient: And then only Criminal,
when either us'd in Excess, by way of En-
couragement to others, &c [u]. He founds
this softning Sense, this · extraordinary
Comment, upon these words of the *Text*
τά ὐκ ἀνήκοντα, *which are not convenient.*
Does St. *Paul* then censure those things only as *inconvenient*, which just before he
declar'd against as not so much as to be
nam'd amongst Christians? Which he had
so earnestly forbidden in the other Places
already cited? To go to the Propriety, and
common acceptation of the Phrase : τά ὐκ
ἀνήκοντα,

[u] *Defence*
of Plays,
p. 22

Ephef. v. 4.

ἀνήκοντα, means thofe Actions which are
foreign, and out of Character, contradi-
ctions to Decency and Duty. And befides,
where the Cafe is fo very plain, and the
Blemifh fo eafily difcover'd, the *Scripture*
does not always ufe the ftrongeft Expreffions in the Prohibition. If Dr. *Filmer*
queftions this Remark, he may find it made
good by the Learned *Hammond* in feveral Inftances ʷ. To thefe I fhall add ᵛ Annot.
one which comes up fully to the prefent in 12 St.
Cafe.
Mat. in C.

St. *Paul* having given a fhort Recital of
the hideous Immorality of the *Heathens* ˣ, ˣ Rom. i.
fubjoyns, that *God gave them over to a* from v. 24,
reprobate Mind, to do thofe things which to 29.
are not convenient, τὰ μὴ καθήκοντα; which
is a perfect equivalent to ἀνήκοντα. Immediately after thefe words, the Apoftle proceeds in the Lift of the Crimes, and tells
us, They were *fill'd with all Unrighteouf-
nefs, Fornication, Wickednefs, Maliciouf-
nefs,* &c. Thus, in St. *Paul's* Language, v. 29. to 32.
the moft flaming Inftances of Vice, the laft
exceffes of Villany, are call'd *things which
are not convenient.*

But notwithftanding the complexion of
the Practice is fo black, the Doctor goes
boldly on in the Caufe, and affirms, *obfcenity is then only declar'd finful by the Apoftle, when either us'd in Excefs, by way of*
encourage-

encouragement to *others*, *or by our* *selves*
set up in competition with our Duty to God ʸ.
When us'd in *excess* ! As if it was allow'd under feveral Degrees and Limita-
tions ! But it may be lie means 'tis then
only exceffive, when *us'd by way of En-*
couragement to others. For the purpofe :
If a Man picks a Pocket, provided 'tis done
only for his own Advantage, without any
defign to propagate the Myftery, and make
the Trade common : Provided the Point
is thus guarded, though it may be *incon-*
venient for the Perfon that lofes his Money, yet there's no manner of Crime in
the Dexterity ! Farther ; either Smut, and
rank Language, is an innocent defenfible practice, or not : If 'tis innocent,
where's the Crime of encouraging others?
What Sin can it be to recommend a fafe
inoffenfive Liberty ? But if 'tis an ill
thing, if 'tis *malum in fe*, how dares any
one venture upon it ? And what Authority has the Doctor to give a Difpenfation ?
And if lufcious and lewd Difcourfe is
highly fcandalous and unchriftian, then certainly we are bound to decline it. From
whence it follows, that thofe who indulge
the Practice, fet up this Liberty *in compe-*
tition with their Duty to God, which is a
Sin even by the Doctor's Confeffion ᶻ

ʸ *Defence of Plays,* p. 22.

ᶻ *Id.* p. 23.

I

I have been the longer upon this Matter, to rescue the *Text* from the Doctor's licentious *Comment*. The wretchedness of the Argument put him upon this desperate Push. He foresaw the *Stage* could be no otherwise defended: He frankly confesses, that unless *Filthiness, obscenity of Speech, and idle Jesting, are admitted, all our Comedies will be swept off.* And thus he seems to boggle at no Expedient, and is resolv'd to maintain his Post at the utmost Hazard. Thus some Men, rather than give up an unwarrantable Diversion, venture to tamper with the Holy *Text*, and wrest it to Loosness and Scandal. Thus the inspir'd Writings are made Ministerial to Vice; and brought to countenance those Liberties which are the Aversions of Natural Conscience, and stand condemn'd by Heathen Sobriety. Can the Doctor expect *Consolation*, as he calls it [a], from such Management as this? And that *the Justice of the Cause* will relieve his Spirits, though *success* should not answer.

To shew the Profaneness of the *Stage,* with respect to Swearing, I quoted St. *Matthew* and St. *James* against this Liberty [b]. *What!* says the Doctor, *is all swearing unlawful? I hope our Author is not turn'd Quaker* [c]. Not at all. I grant an assurance of fair Dealing, and putting an end

Marginal notes:
P. 20.

a Pref. p. 11.
  Ibid.

b Matth. v.
  James v.
  First Defence of the View *in* Answer *to the* Amendments, &c.
  P. 134.
c Dr. Filmer, p. 28.

Heb. vi. 16. *end to Strife*, is a very defensible Motive for such an Expedient. But are there any Affidavits to be made upon the *Stage*, any Titles to be try'd , any *Treaties* to be sign'd and ratify'd ? Is there any occasion for the discovery of Truth, the Tryal of Malefactors, or doing Right to the Publick Interest ? Now these, and such like, are the only justifiable grounds for swearing. But when an Oath is unnecessary, it comes under the *Gospel* Prohibition, and is certainly a Crime. But the Doctor is of another mind ; he makes no scruple to affirm, That *when a wicked Wretch swears upon the Stage, 'tis not taking God's Name in vain ; nor implies any contempt of his* Majesty [d]. His Reason is, because the *Man is punish'd for his Misbehaviour, and made Guilty for a warning [c] to others.* At this rate a Man may have a *Patent* for the *Highway* , provided he is but secur'd to *Justice*, and forth-coming for the Gallows. 'Tis no matter for his taking a Purse, and making bold with the *Constitution*, and committing Murther upon the Road : Let him but be hang'd in *Terrorem*, and People have the Benefit of seeing him suffer, and all's well enough. But I have reply'd to this Objection already, and shall consider it no farther [e].

However, the Doctor supposes *an Oath or two , or it may be more* , may be put in

the

[d] *Defence of Plays,* p. 28, 31. *Ibid.*

[e] *Reply to the Amendments,* p. 15 *Second Defence of the View, &c.* p. 60.

the Mouth of an Atheift, without any manner of Profanenefs [f]. This is a moft admirable Provifion to fecure the *Franchifes* of the *Stage* ! But then the Doctor is fo fcrupulous, as not to allow a *Stage Bully* to lard every Sentence, and fwear upon the ftretch [g].

[f] *Dr. Filmer, p.* 28, 32.

[g] *Id.* p. 69.

By the Doctor's Divinity, one would think there was a certain number of Oaths requir'd, to the making a Man criminal. But I believe every body will find the Effence of Sin confifts in the Obliquity of the Act, in the Tranfgreffion of the Law, and in going off from the Rule of Duty. 'Tis true, the Repetition of an ill thing, heightens the Degree, and inflames the Guilt, but does not affect the Quality of the Practice.

But *Stage*-fwearing is only to make a profane Character more *lively* and *natural,* and therefore mayn't an *Oath or two pafs* [h] ? By this Argument, when a Man is to dye in *Tragedy,* he fhould be kill'd in earneft. For to fee him agonizing, and weltring in his Blood, would heighten the Action extremely, and affect the Company to an unufual Degree. This fighting in earneft made the *Gladiators* more agreeable to the Romans : Thus unlefs there's Mifchief done at a *Prize,* the Fencers are rail'd on, and the Company think themfelves cheated. And therefore to illuftrate the Matter farther ; If the Deftruction

[h] *Ibid.*

ͳion of *Troy* was to be reprefented, though we muft not go the length of *Nero*'s Fancy, and fet the *Town* in a Blaze : Nay, probably the Doctor is fo fcrupulous as not to admit the laying all *Drury-lane*, and the *Hay-market* in Afhes. But then fetting Fire to the *Stage*, and burning a Houfe *or two*, *or it may be more*, as he has it, would be very neceffary to give Truth and Spirit to the Performance.

Thefe Inftances, I hope, may ferve to difentangle the Doctor's Underftanding. For if the Plea of Imitation, and Dramatick Intereft, won't excufe Murther and burning of Houfes, why fhould Profanenefs pretend to this *Liberty ?* I don't fay fwearing an Oath is as bad as committing Murther : But this I affirm, that fwearing is a profane Liberty, 'tis an Infolence upon God Almighty ; 'tis a breach of Law Divine and Humane. And this is fufficient to make the Inftance parallel, and give force to the Comparifon. Now if common fwearing is Wicked and Irreligious in other Places, how comes it to be inoffenfive in the *Play-Houfe ?* Have the *Poets* a difcharge from the Duties of Religion, and a Privilege to infult their *Maker ?*

Well ! though the Doctor can't produce their *Exemption*, he'll endeavour to ferve them another way. If the Penalties of Religion can't be taken off, he'll try to cover

them

and Profaneneſs? What makes him clog their Humour, and tye them up to an Oath or two [n]? He lets his *Lyars* go at large, and neither ſtints them in Quality or Number. His reſtraint therefore upon *Swearing* is a plain Confeſſion of the diſparity of the Caſe.

But the Poets don't ſpeak their own ſenſe [o]. That ſignifies nothing: I have told him already, that he who makes a Man mad, muſt anſwer for his diſtraction [p].

His ſaying the *Poets Heart does not go along with their Pen*; if 'tis true, is quite ſhort of a Defence [q]. Whether the Doctor knows it or not, the *Pen* is a dangerous Weapon, if untowardly manag'd; and has ruin'd many a one, though neither their *Heart*, nor their *Head*, has gone along with it. To illuſtrate the Matter.

What if a Man ſigns away his *Eſtate*, or ſets his Hand to a *Plot*, without thinking? Will the Plea of his Folly indemnifie him? If the *Poets* will venture to make ſport with Profaneneſs, reſign their Conſcience to their Intereſt, and gratifie Libertines at the expence of Religion, they muſt account for their Miſbehaviour. And though the *Stage-Poets* are not always bound *to ſpeak their own Sentiments* [r], yet to ſwear, or blaſpheme in Fiction, is much more than is allow'd. His Inſtance therefore

4 Si

Marginal notes:
*Idem.
p. 28, 69.

Id. p. 30.

Reply to
Relap-
p. 108.
efence
lays,

them from the *Law*. For if he can but ſecure them from *Indictments*, he concludes their Conſciences will ſhift well enough.

For this purpoſe, he puts them in a way to carry on their Profaneneſs in defiance of the *Statute*. Let them but forbear the mention of the Name of God, and ſome other few Inſtances, and the *Act* can't touch them [i]. As much as to ſay, the Diverſion of Oaths, and Curſing, is not ſo mightily cramp'd as ſome People fancy. Let them but ſwear with Diſcretion, and they are ſafe enough! For, as he obſerves, ſome of our *Poets ſwear frequently by Heaven, and ſometimes too by Hell*; and yet he *can't ſee how either of thoſe Oaths, or any other of the like Nature, are forbidden by this Act*. I believe he may ſee it if he pleaſes: For has not our Saviour told us, That he *that ſwears by Heaven, ſwears by the Throne of God, and by him that ſits thereon*. I hope the Doctor does not think our *Legiſlators* queſtion'd the Authority of this Reſolution: And if not, the ſwearing by *Heaven* muſt fall under the diſcountenance of the *Act*, and come within the compaſs of the Prohibition.

The Doctor's next attempt is, to gloſs away the meaning of the *Statute*, and make it ſignifie nothing. *There is not the leaſt mention*, ſays he, *made in this Act, either*

B *of*

Marginal notes:
3 Jac. 1.
cap. 21.

[i] *Defence of Plays.*
p. 33.

Ibid.

S. Mat. xxiii.
22.

of direct, or indirect swearing; and how then

[k] *Defence of Plays, P. 34.* *is it forbidden* [k] *?* Not forbidden ! Does not the *Act* declare against the **great Abuse of the Holy Name of God in Stage-plays ?** And is not the Name of God abus'd in common swearing ? Not abus'd, when the Divine Majesty is made bold with, to shew the contempt of his Power, to attest Trifles, and grace an intemperate Passion ?

He has another reserve, and argues, That *the use of the Name of God on the* Stage *is no otherwise prohibited, than as it may be*
[l] *Ibid.* *jestingly, or profanely abus'd there* [l]. By this Gentleman's favour, the *Act* supposes the *Play-houses* all Sport and Diversion ; and that the Name of God can't be mention'd there without Jest and Prophanation. For what are *Plays* but Buffooning, Fiction, and Farce, design'd for the entertainment of the *Audience ?*

But though the *Stage* is in Jest, the *Law* is in Earnest : And that his *reading* upon the *Statute* won't pass in *Westminster-Hall*, the *Players* can satisfie him from their own Experience. He pretends, *I may as well tax our Poets with the sin of Lying, as that of Swearing, because they vent a great many untruths in their Dramatick Chara-*
[m] *Id. p. 30.* *cters* [m]. To this Cavil 'tis sufficient to return, that the Instance is by no means parallel.

parallel. He may as well say, because Falshood and failing in Honour, may pass upon the *Stage* with Discipline at the end on't ; therefore the *Players* may Stab and Pistol one another ! For since the *Poet* does not fight in Person, since the Men are destroy'd in Jest, and die only like *Gladiators*, to divert the Company, all's well enough.

Secondly, Lying is a Fault, because makes the Marks of *Speech* insignifica, stroys Trust between Man and Ma weakens the Interest of *Society*. B Truth is known to be strain'd only and the Lyar suffers by the Lib no body is deceiv'd, or encoura thus the Sting is pull'd out, and nity prevented.

But some practices are intol every Circumstance : Like pretence of inward Dislike Representation, of Jest, or excuse them. And of thi is one. 'Tis an out-rage a bold Contempt of the g bare pronouncing make Guilt sticks upon the Sin in the Sound. Th what sensible of thi Reason else does he *Atheists* from their

Sir *John Denham*, and my Lord *Orrery*, is
quite wide of his purpose. For if the *Persons* in the *Sophy*, or *Mustapha*, had droll'd
upon the *Trinity*, or burlesqu'd the four
Gospels, the cover of a Turkish Character
would have been a lamentable Excuse. And
though we could not conclude the *Authors
Mahometans* from this management, yet we
might think them *Atheists*, and that's
worse [f]. Nay, give the Doctor but leave [f] *Id. p. 31,*
to write on, and forget himself, and we
shall find him come out with the same
Truth, without much mincing the matter.
Towards the latter end of his *Book* [t], he [t] *Id. p. 152,*
lets us know, 'tis probable the *Heathen Stage* 153.
*expos'd the Christian Faith, and made merry
with the most sacred Mysteries.* For this
reason, says the Doctor, the *Fathers* stood
aloof in their Satyr, and only *hinted the
Profaneness.* To this reservedness they were
oblig'd, in Reverence to Religion: For, as
he continues, *they could not enlarge upon
such hellish practices without Horror.* And
if the *Fathers* declin'd repeating profane
Discourse, and ought to do it, as the Doctor
argues; I say, if they declin'd the mention
of Profaneness, though in order to stigma-
tize and detest it; can we imagine they
would have resign'd it to Pleasure, and allow'd it for Diversion?

He

He tells me, I charge only fix *Plays*
Id. p. 26. with fwearing ᵘ : But this is a Miftake, as
ᵛ *See Pre-* the Doctor might eafily have difcover'd ᵂ.
face to the
firft Defence
of the View,
&c.
He is not pleas'd with my reprefenting
Swearing in the *Play-Houfe*, as a breach
of good breeding to the Women ˣ. But
ˣ *Defence*
of Plays,
p. 34.
if Swearing before Women is ill Manners
in other Places, why not upon the *Stage ?*
How come the *Players* to be difcharg'd from
common Decency ? The Doctor pretends,
Ib. & p.36.
the *Actors*, and the *Ladies*, *don't make the
fame Company*. By his favour, though they
don't addrefs the *Ladies*, excepting in the
Prologue and *Epilogue*, yet they are within fight and hearing. And thus the *Dialogue* paffing all under the *Ladies* notice,
the *Actors* are ty'd to the common Rules
of Decorum. 'Tis true, the Doctor is of
another mind ; but what if the Ladies are
fo nice, as not to be of his Opinion ? What
if they have fo much Confcience, as not
to think themfelves diverted with Curfing,
Swearing, and other fcandalous Behaviour ?
Why then he frankly tells them, They
muft e'en ftay at Home, *and wave the Di-*
ʸ P. 36.
verfion of the Theatre ʸ. For unlefs they
can entertain themfelves with *Bullies* and
Proftitutes, *acting* in the fcandal of their
Character, they muft be very much difap-
pointed by the *Players*. The arguing a-
ᶻ P. 37.
gainft this Liberty, he calls *wretched Stuff* ᶻ,
and

and complains, the *Stage* will be quite ruin'd by such restraints ᵃ : That is to say, *P. 38.* they must either do Mischief, or nothing.

But after all, the Doctor is not easie under his distinctions about *Swearing* : He *doubts he may be blam'd for what he has said upon the subject, and represented as a favourer of this Vice* ᵇ. Truly I think his *Pref. p.9.* apprehensions are very reasonable: But how does he disengage himself? He *desires the Reader to take notice, that he no where recommends the use of it to our Poets.* But since he allows it upon *extraordinary occasions* ᶜ, *Preface, p. 10.* and leaves the regulation to the *Poet's* Conscience ; since he takes pains to shew the convenience, and argues in Defence of the practice ; since he makes no scruple of going these lengths, what signifies his Declaration ? All this demureness amounts to no more than *protestatio contra Factum* ; disclaiming his own Act, and renouncing that in the *Preface*, which he maintains in the *Book.*

To proceed. The Doctor will have it, the *Argument* led me to engage the *Libertine* ; and that I should have shewn no pretence of *Stage*-Discipline would have atton'd for the Smut and Profaneness in that *Play*, But, it seems, *the Catastrophe was there too exemplary and terrible for my purpose* ᵈ. ᵈ *Pag. 43, 44, 45.*

To this I answer:

B 4   First,

Firſt, That I have already perform'd what the Doctor requires. I have ſhewn in general, that no Stage Diſcipline, though never ſo ſevere, will juſtifie the repreſentation of *Smut* and *Profaneneſs* [e].

Secondly, If I had happen'd to have been ſhort in this matter, the Doctor could have ſupply'd that defect. For he grants, the *Comick Poet ought not to fly out into the groſſeſt extravagancies of Smut, under the pretence of repreſenting a Whore, or a Pimp: Nor the Tragick Poet fly in the Face of Heaven, and blaſpheme at any rate, under the protection of Stage Diſcipline* [f]. By theſe Rules he has plainly condemn'd the *Libertine*, notwithſtanding the Juſtice and *Terror of the Cataſtrophe*. For this *Play*, by his own Confeſſion, *has three times as much Smut, Profaneneſs, and Blaſphemy, as any Stage performance* cited by me [g]. This *Play* then has *gone to the extent of an* Atheiſtick *Character* [h]. The ſtrokes are groſs, and dawb'd all over the *Piece*, and not *ſparingly, nicely,* and *carefully manag'd,* as the Doctor preſcribes [i]. And yet after all, he is ſo frank as to declare, that if I had attack'd this *Play* with ſucceſs, I *had ſhaken the very Foundation of the Play-Houſe, and gain'd an abſolute Victory* [k]. Now the Doctor has done this buſineſs for me, and made the attempt unneceſſary. No Gun-powder **could**

Marginal notes:

[e] *Short View, &c.* p. 96. *Firſt Defence of the View, &c.* p. 8, *to* 18.

[f] *Defence of Plays,* p. 62.

[g] *Id.* p. 43.

[h] *Id.* p. 69.

[i] *Ibid.*

[k] *Id.* p. 45.

could blow up the *Theatre* more effectually than thefe Conceffions and Maxims laid down by this Gentleman.

He urges the Profanenefs of *Prometheus*, and *Ajax*, in *Æfchylus* and *Sophocles:* He obferves the *Short View*, &c. excufes the reprefentation of thefe Sallies upon the fcore of *Stage* Difcipline : From hence he infers, a Chriftian *Stage Poet* may take the fame liberty [1].

To this it may be return'd,

Firft, That the Character of the Heathen Gods was foul and blemifh'd : This circum-ftance made the liberty taken with them more excufeable.

Secondly, Heathens and Chriftians are un-der a different Regulation ; for this reafon we can't argue for the fame Latitude from one to the other. Different rules alter the nature of Duty, and oblige to a different Practice [m]. To which I may add, that the Doctor owns the *Fathers could not enlarge on the blafphemies of the Heathens without Horror* [n].

The Doctor goes on, and lets us know how tender he is of the *Play-Houfe* intereft, and what we are to expect from his *Refor-mation*. He is refolv'd to deal gently with them, and leave them a ftock of their old *Commodities* to trade with. He lays it down for a Maxim, that if *Smut* and *Profanenefs* can't

[1] *Id.* p. 46. to 50.

[m] *Short View, &c.* p. 14. *Second De-fence of the View, &c.* p. 107.

[n] *Defence of Plays*, p. 153.

can't be allow'd, the *Poets muſt have few, or* *no Characters to practice on* °. Theſe things it ſeems are neceſſary Ingredients of Diverſion, and Fundamental to the ſatisfaction of Mankind. But then to varniſh over the matter, he tells us, *Smut muſt not be out of Character, or too groſs in Terms or Senſe :* But *when 'tis wrap'd up in clean Linen, and lies in double Entendres, 'tis eaſie and natural,* and he *ſees no great danger in it* ᴾ. It may be ſo ! However, *Livy* was not at a of the Doctor's mind �q. I'm ſorry to find this *Chriſtian Reformer* fall ſhort of *Pagan* Virtue.

But to make the Indulgence more ſignificant, the Doctor out of his great Courteſie, has left the regulation of this matter with the *Poets :* They are to ſtate the Proportion ; to ſettle the Doſe, and weigh out the Scruples. But why muſt the *Audience* be entertain'd with *Smut,* convey'd with Advantage ? Is it to make the Poiſon more palatable ; to make the Attack more under cover, and convey the Infection with leſs Infamy ? Theſe are bad deſigns. *Smut* under any diſguiſe, is inconſiſtent with the ſobriety of Religion : *Evil Communication corrupts good Manners.* Theſe are ſome of the *unfruitful works of darkneſs,* with which we are forbidden to have *any Fellowſhip.* I can't help putting the Queſtion again : This

Smut

Id. p.61.

ᴮ *Id.* p.65.

ᵠ Inſtitut. l. 6. c. 3.

1 Cor. xv. 33. Epheſ. v. 11.

Smut thus drefs'd and varnifh'd, to what purpofe is it us'd? For the benefit of Inftruction? That won't do. His anfwer muft be, 'tis to pleafe the *Audience*, and give Spirit to the Entertainment. That is in other words, 'tis to folicite the Fancy, and awaken the Folly of the Paffions. Now there's no need of Suggeftion and Incitement: People are apt to run too faft of themfelves, and like *Phaeton's* Horfes,

——Labor eft inhibere volantes.

Abftinence and Mortification has formerly been thought neceffary for the fecurity of Virtue : What elfe is the meaning of the Difcipline and Fafting prefcrib'd by the Church? What made fo many holy Men retreat to Solitude, but only to get out of the way of Temptation? But by the Doctor's Indulgence, one would think humane Nature was ftrangely mended ; that our Reafon was grown more abfolute, and we had nothing of the Weaknefs of former Ages about us.

He allows the *Comick Poets difguifed Oaths, becaufe they are in reality nothing but infignificant by-words, taken up for the moft part by good People, to avoid Swearing* [r]. Can't good People then avoid Swearing, without talking Nonfenfe? If there's no fignifica-

[r] *Defence of Plays, p. 65.*

tion

tion within thefe Forms of Speech, to what
purpofe fhould the *Poet* lard his Difcourfe
with them? Do words without meaning recommend Converfation? 'Tis plain therefore, they are taken for Oaths, and that the
Relifh proceeds from the Profanenefs; And
if the Doctor did not think fo, I can't fee
why he fhould infift fo much upon the Liberty.

As for his alledging the Practice of good
Men, and concluding their Judgment from
thence; 'tis fufficient to reply, That the
moft unexceptionable People never ufe thefe
difguis'd Oaths : And as for the *good Men,*
if there is any fuch, who venture thus far,
'tis certainly no part of their Goodnefs.

He thinks it hard meafure not to allow
Profanenefs on the *Stage*, *under any pre-*
tence of Character or Difcipline [s]. I would
defire him to anfwer my Reafons, before he
makes this Complaint. But he excepts a-
gainft an Expedient of mine, with reference
to this matter. The Paffage ftands thus.
To fay a Man has been profane in general,
and then to punifh him, is fomewhat intelligi-
ble [t]. What *can be more ridiculous*, fays
the Doctor, *than this piece of dramatick Ju-*
ftice? How is it poffible to diftinguifh the
Character of an Atheift, from a Man of Re-
ligion, but by fomething in his Difcourfe [u]?
Does the Doctor then believe, that unlefs a
Malefactor

[s] *Id.* p. 70.

[t] *Firft De-fence of the View,* &c. p. 16.

[u] *Defence of Plays,* p. 70, 71.

Malefactor repeats his Crimes at his **Tryal,**
or at leaft the Hiftory of them, the *Court*
has no Power to punifh? But making *a Man
an Example without Inftance, or particula-
"ity, is judging without Procefs, condemning
without Proof, and the greateft Injuftice imaginable* ʷ.   It feems good Witnefs ftands ᵛ *Ibid.*
for nothing with the Doctor.   By this arguing, unlefs a *Juftice* fees a Pick-pocket
practife before him, he has no Authority to
make his *Mittimus.*   And thus, if a Malefactor is indicted for Murther, unlefs the
Jurors are Eye-witneffes of the Fact, they
are upon no account to bring him in Guilty.   But the Doctor is in a great Fright, for
fear my *Theatral piece of Juftice fhould become National,* and then the Cafe would be
fad ˣ.   For if fallies of Profanenefs, if a-ˣ *P.* 72.
theiftick and blafphemous Rants are not allow'd to prove the Crime, and make a dramatick Malefactor, the confequence may
prove Mortal to the Nation.   How fo?
Why, unlefs this liberty is taken, *who can
fecure us, but that it may be many an honeft
Man's Fate to be condemn'd by Report, and
hang'd by Hearfay* ʸ?
                                                            ʸ *Ibid.*
By this fhrewd Objection one would ima-
gine the *Theatre* was the Standard of *Law,*
and that the *ruled* cafes in *Tragedy* were
more to be regarded than St. *Germain's Maxims,* or the *Precedents* in *Coke.*   'Tis true,
the

the Infection of the *Play-Houfe* reaches a
great way, and poifons abundance of People;
but for all that I can't believe it has feiz'd
the Courts of *Juftice*, and left the *Tokens*
upon *Weftminfter-Hall*. However, if *Plays*
have fuch a dangerous Afcendant, and carry
fuch a force of Malignity, I fhould think
the beft fecurity would be to keep out
of harm's way, and ftand clear of that Diverfion.

The Doctor argues, That *if the bare re-*
peating any thing profane, &c. is a Sin, then
my Collection of Smut, of blafphemous and
z Id. p.73, atheiftical Stuff, is not to be excus'd z. But
74. if the citing all thefe Inftances of Scandal
and Profanenefs is juftifiable in the *Short*
View, &c. If the Cenfure and Correction is
a warrant for producing the ill Sight, why
may not the *Stage* Poets take the fame liberty? To this I anfwer.

Firft, That the Doctor mifreports Matter
of Fact: For as to Smut and Oaths, thefe
fcandalous Paffages are purpofely declin'd;
there's only a reference to the *Play*, and
Page, to juftifie the Charge.

Secondly, As to *Profanenefs*, the cafe is
not parallel. Had I made the profane Paffages, it had been to the Doctor's purpofe;
but I produce nothing but what has been
written by the *Poets*, *Acted* on the *Stage*,
and ftands publickly in Print. Now there's

great

great difference between finding a Malefactor, and making one. When a Wretch
once appears, and grows infectious, 'tis neceffary to mark him for Terror, that the
Punifhment may be as publick as the Crime:
But then 'tis only the neceffity which can
juftifie the tryal of fuch Offendors: Now
the *Poets* are under no fuch neceffity; for
what neceffity can they have, unlefs that of
Intereft, to reprefent a Villain?

On the other hand ; To let Libertines
and Atheifts droll upon Religion, and blu-
fter out Blafphemy and Defiance : To do
this under pretence to make them fmart
for't, is a dangerous Experiment ; fuch a
contrivance is like bringing a Difeafe into
a Town, for the fake of trying ones Skill in
curing it. But 'tis plain, he that ufes this
Method makes a Property of his *Patient*,
and prefcribes to nothing but his own Pocket. To give Poifon, to fhew the ftrength
of an Antidote, is the Trick of a Mounte-
bank ; the Body fuffers in the Conteft, and
fomething of the Mifchief often remains.

The Doctor's next attempt is to prove an
inconfiftency between my *Short View*, &c.
and my *Firft Defence*. In the latter, I had
obferv'd, *That the* Play-Houfe *often fpreads
thofe Vices it reprefents, and that the Hu-
mour of the Town is learn'd by fhewing it* ². ² Defence of
How, fays the Doctor, *are thofe Vices re-* the View,
prefented &c. p.

*prefented on the Stage, the Humour of the
Town! This plainly contradicts what Mr.* Collier *has very confidently afferted in his* View,
that it was the Stage *which poifon'd the*
Town ; *whereas, by what he here fays, we
muft conclude, that it was the* Town *rather*
[b] Defence of *that debauch'd the* Stage [b] Whether the
Plays, *Confidence* lies in the *View,* or in the Doctor,
p. 75. the *Reader* muft judge. But then as to
the Argument, I fay ftill, that the *Stage*
has poifon'd the *Town,* and *Country* too :
That their ftirring offenfive Humours, *reading* upon an infectious Body, and diffecting
the Plague, helps to fpread the Contagion,
and make the Difeafe more Epidemical.
Thus the *Play-Houfe* propagates its firft Mifchief, reaches farther into the Nation, and
improves the Vices of the Age: And where's
the contradiction in all this?

The Doctor agrees in the main with the
fourth Chapter in the *View,* &c. and very
honeftly grants, the Clergy ought by no
means to be *maltraited* and ridicul'd on the
[c] Id. p. 82. *Stage* [c].

But after all this Civility, the Doctor can't
help difcovering his partiality to the *Stage :*
For what reafon elfe does he beftow three
or four pages to juftifie the *Poet*'s Conduct
in *Œdipus?* When he does as good as own
[d] Id. p. 83. the Difpute is nothing to his purpofe [d]. His
Objections againft my Remarks on this Paf-
fage,

fage, he might have found anfwer'd in my
fecond *Defence* of the *View* [e], &c. and thither I refer him.

I ftill affirm, notwithftanding the Doctor's
cavil, that *Plays*, where the Argument and
Manner are religious and folemn, are *Acted*
in Monafteries in *France*, and in other
Countries too : And that the Fact ftands
thus, the Doctor upon enquiry may fatisfie
himfelf.

But the Doctor is difpleas'd with my not
allowing the *Stage* the Liberty of acting a
religious Play [f]. In defence of this practice
he alledges *Corneille*'s *Polyeucte* on the *Theatre* at *Paris*. He may remember, that the
French *Stage*, though far fhort of the Scandal of the *Englifh*, lay under the Cenfure
of the Church, and the *Players* were refus'd
the *Sacrament* [g]. Indeed the *acting* a religious *Play* upon the modern *Theatre*, would
be next to a Libertine's preaching in a
Houfe of *Proftitution*; where the Place, and
the Perfon, is enough to burlefque the Difcourfe, and almoft make the *Text* Apocry-
phal : For this reafon, as the Doctor confeffes, there was a mighty noife made againft
Moliere's *Faux Devot*. The ground of the
Cenfure lay upon the *Stage*'s Prefumption,
in medling with *Sacred* and *Religious Matters* [h]. 'Tis true, the Doctor tells us this
noife was made by *fome certain Bigots*. But

[e] *Reply to the Ancient and Modern Stages furvey'd, p. 63, 64.*

[f] *Defence of Plays, p. 90.*

[g] *Short View, &c. p. 247, 248.*

[h] *Defence of Plays, p. 90.*

C   to

to give Men of Confcience and Piety an ill
Name, is an eafie way of anfwering. But

ⁱ *Ibid.* *Moliere vindicates* his *Play* ⁱ. *Moliere's* manner was Licentious, and his Authority fig-
nifies nothing. As for his Arguments, they
are either drawn from *Pagan* Cuftoms, from
unrefembling Cafes, or Precedents liable to
exception.

The Doctor would gladly difprove my
Exceptions againft the *Stage*, for making
ᵏ *Id.* p. 95. too bold with *Quality* ᵏ. But here, after a
little Fluttering and Fencing with a *Mar-
quis*, and bringing fome difabled Objections
on the Board ; after a little flourifh to difcover his good will, he retires within the
Lines, gives up the Point, owns the *Poet's*
oblig'd to treat the *Coronets* with more regard, and not to expofe the Nobility in ri-
ˡ *Id.* p. 100, diculous Characters ˡ.
101.

His laft attack is upon the Authorities
cited in the fixth *Chapter* of the *Short View*,
&c. And here he feems to have tranfcrib'd
the Objections made by Mr. *Dennis*, and the
Author of the *Ancient and Modern Stages*
ᵐ *Id.* p. 102. *furvey'd* ᵐ. What has been offer'd by both
& dein. thefe Adverfaries , I have anfwer'd long
fince; and maintain'd the Teftimonies both
as to Pertinency, and fairnefs of Citation.
And that nothing material might be omited,
my *fecond Defence* has more than fifty pages
upon

upon this Argument [n]. Now tho' this laft
Book has undertaken almoft all Dr. *Filmer's*
exceptions, and was publifh'd in 1699, yet
he takes no manner of notice of it. This
Conduct is very furprizing ; the beft thing
I can fay for him is, that he never faw my
Reply to Dr. *Drake*. This I confefs is but
a poor excufe : Had the Doctor's enquiry
been moderately careful, I fancy he might
have fpar'd the pains of his *Book*. However, fince he has given me fo little trouble, this grofs overfight of his may be the
better pafs'd over. I muft now confider
thofe few fupplemental Remarks, advanc'd
in defence of the *Stage*.

In the firft place, he endeavours to weak-
en the Authority of the Philofophers, Hi-
ftorians, and other *Pagan* Writers of Figure,
who have cenfur'd the *Stage*.

To do execution upon this quarter, he
fuppofes *Plays* were *acted* in the Countries
where this Complaint was preferr'd againft
them. This liberty of *acting* he infers, a-
mounts to an Allowance and Approbation of
the *higher Powers* [o] ; and that the publick
Allowance is an overbalance, to the diflike
of a few private Men, tho' never fo confider-
able [p] : And thus, by putting the *Stage* under the Protection of the Magiftracy of *Italy*
and *Greece*, he thinks there is no coming at
them. But all this pretence of publick Coun-

[n] See Reply to the Vindicator of the Relapfe, p. 132. to p. 139. Second Defence of the View, p. 4. to p. 56.

[o] Defence of Plays, p. 103.

[p] Ibid. & p. 104.

tenance ;

tenance ; this shew of the Roman *Legions* is nothing but false *Muster*. For,

First, I have already prov'd the *Stage* has been discountenanc'd and suppress'd in some of the most famous Governments, and never admitted in others ᑫ.

Secondly, I desire him to consider, whether Connivance can be reasonably construed to Approbation ? The *State* sometimes indulges those liberties which we can't suppose the *Legislature* would ever recommend, or justifie. The Doctor knows the *Stews* have been publickly suffer'd in *England*, and are now allow'd, as he calls it, in some Countries of *Europe*. But to conclude from hence, that those Governments declare Whoredom no Sin, and make Lewdness part of the *Constitution*, would be a most unjust Censure.

To proceed. I cited two *Acts* of *Parliament* to shew how much the *Stage* stands discountenanc'd by our own *Constitution* ʳ. The *Statutes* the Doctor confesses would have been *very patt to my purpose, had I not left out two very material words, absolutely necessary to the right understanding of the Law* ʳ. And now where lies the Crime of misreporting ? 'Tis only in not reciting the words 𝖜𝖆𝖓𝖉𝖗𝖎𝖓𝖌 𝕬𝖇𝖗𝖔𝖆𝖉. And is this such a hideous omission ? The Doctor says yes. For from hence it appears, 'tis not

ᑫ *Second Defence of the View, from* p. 4c. *to* p 56.

ʳ Eliz. 39. c. 4. 1 Jac. 1. c. 7. *View,* p. 241.

ʳ *Defence of Plays,* p. 124.

4 *the*

the *Player*, but the *Stroller*, and the *Vaga-
bond*, that is cenfur'd by this *Law* ; (mean-
ing the firft *Statute*) [f]. Does the Doctor [f] *Id.* p.125,
then think the *Players* are barr'd the conve- 126, 127.
nience of taking a Journey? Muft they not
vifit their Friends, and folicite their Affairs in the Country? To throw them thus
out of common liberty, is more than the
Law will allow him. Let but the *Stage* be
left behind, and they may make the Tour
of the Ifland, and take their Range with
fafety enough. But if they travell'd in the
diftinctions of their Character, fet up their
Trade, and carry'd their Diverfion along
with them ; in this cafe they were look'd
on as a *Nufance*, and lay terribly expos'd.
From whence nothing can be plainer, than
that the Penalty of the *Act* is pointed againft
the *Myftery*, ftrikes full upon the *Bufinefs*,
and reaches the *Players* under that precife
denomination.

The Doctor, to make all fure, fays the
*Statute is expir'd, and has been out of Doors
above threefcore Years* [t]. But then his Cou- [t] *Ibid.*
rage does not hold ; he is at a lofs about the
Point, and fomewhat afraid the two *Statutes*
are ftill in force. However, he hopes the Privilege of licenfing *Players*, which is taken
from the *Peers* by the latter *Act*, does not
affect the *Crown* [u] : And thus he cafts about [u] *Ibid.*
for a farther Protection, retreats to the *Pre-*

C 3 *rogative*,

rogative, and leaves the *Stage* under the Cannon of *Whitehall*. Well! To give him a lift for once, I grant thefe *Acts are out of Doors*; but what's all this to the Doctor's Advantage? Were they not once part of the *Conftitution*, and the Senfe of the Wifdom of the Nation? And if fo, is not this fufficient for my purpofe in citing them?

I obferv'd in the *View*, &c. that the Magiftracy of *London* addrefs'd Queen *Elizabeth* in *Council*, for leave to pull down the *Play-Houfes* within the *City*; that their Petition was granted, and the *Play-Houfes* pull'd down ^w. It feems thefe Gentlemen were ftrongly apprehenfive, that the Intereft of the City, and *Theatre*, were inconfiftent with each other: That thefe Diverfions would lay Induftry afleep, and difable the purfuits of Wealth, and Honour: That this was the way to throw Bufinefs and Sobriety out of young People's Heads, and leave them neither Money nor Morals: That when the Lufcioufnefs of the Dialogue, the Mufick, and gayety of the Place has once feiz'd and fubdu'd their Fancy, they are feldom good for any thing but to repeat their fatisfaction at a Tavern; to ftart an Intreague, or rob their Mafter's Cafh. This is the fenfe of the *Cities* Petition; and by the Iffue of the Matter, it feems the *Queen* and *Council* were much of the fame Opinion.

Short View, &c. p. 242, 243.

nion. And now which way does the Doctor
make this Inſtance unſerviceable ? He does
not deny, but that the *Play-Houſes* were
pull'd down : *But then*, ſays he, *what of
all that ? Is it ſuch a wonder that a wiſe
and gracious Queen ſhould leave the Government of the City to the pious Lord Mayor,
and his ſanctified Brethren ?* For all this odd [x] *Defence
of Plays,*
Jeſt upon *Guildhall*, it ſeems this permiſſion p. 129.
was an Inſtance of her Majeſties Wiſdom.
Upon ſecond Thoughts, he won't allow this
neither. *For the Queen, wiſe as ſhe was,
could not foreſee the dangerous conſequence of
ſuch an Indulgence.* Very likely ! For a
Prince muſt be unuſually ſharp ſighted, to
foreſee the danger of diſcouraging Idleneſs,
and putting a ſtop to Immorality ! But the
Doctor won't be taken in this ſenſe. He is
throughly convinc'd, this diſcouraging the
*Stage, and ſome other Royal Condeſcenſions of
the like Nature* [y], gave a mortal Blow to the [y] *One of
this other
Condeſcenti-
ons, was
putting
down the
Gaming
Houſes.*
[z] *Idem.
p. 130.*
Nation. This countenance from Court rais'd
the Reputation of the *Puritanical* Faction,
and put them in a condition to *diſpute with*
King James, *and fight King* Charles [z]. It ſeems
'tis dangerous Buſineſs to check the ſallies of
Licence and Folly ; 'tis enough to pull a
Government in pieces : For if People muſt
not be *Rakes*, they will certainly be Rebels!

In anſwer to my Authorities from the Primitive Church, the Doctor replies, that ſix

of

of my seven *Councils* are nothing to the
purpose ^a. Under favour, two of them by
his own suppofition, are full to the purpofe ^b. But why are the *Councils* foreign
to the Point? *Becaufe*, fays the Doctor,
they are levell'd againft the Players, not
Plays; *againft the Calling, not the thing it
felf* ^c. Granting his suppofition, how does
this difable the Exception, and make the
Teftimony foreign? For are not our *Play-
Houfes* as much within a Calling as any
other Employment? Don't the *Actors* profefs the bufinefs of the *Stage*, and live and
die in that *Myftery?* If therefore, as the
Doctor confefles, the *Councils* condemn the
Calling of *Players:* If this be fo, the Difcipline of the Church bears down upon our
Age and Country, and ftrikes the *Englifh*,
no lefs than the *Roman* Theatre.

However, if there's no Relief to be expected from this Quarter, the Doctor can
apply to Modern Protection: And here
Bifhop *Sanderfon* is brought to vouch the
Lawfulnefs of the *Stage Calling*. Let us
fee then how far this Learned Cafuift ferves
the purpofe: He affirms, That *he will not
fay the Calling is unlawful*. And then having advis'd the *Players* to examine, *whether they might not have been better employ'd
in another way; and what weight there is
in the Motives which determin'd them to this
Employ-*

^a *Idem*,
p. 136.

^b Viz.*Third
Council of
Carthage,
and fecond
Council of
Chaalons.
See View,
&c. p. 250,
251.*

^c *Defence
of Plays*,
p. 136.

Employment. After this Advice, I fay, he leaves the decifion to their Confciences, and concludes, *If their own Hearts condemn them not, neither do I* [d]. To this I anfwer,

Firft, That the Bifhop, as Dr. *Filmer* cites him, declares pofitively, *That if the Play-ers fhould have been tryed by the Bench of Fathers and Councils of Old, or would have put it to the moft Voices among later Di-vines, both Popifh and Reform'd, they had been all utterly caft, and condemn'd——moft holding not the Calling only, but the Practice, and Thing it felf, unlawful, and damnable* [e].

Now what will the Doctor gain by this Teftimony? He has only brought the Bifhop into *view*, to make a fingular Figure, and be overlay'd with numbers: For not-withftanding the advantage of this Prelate's Memory, I conceive impartial Judges will not believe him a Counter-poife to the *Fa-thers* and *Councils :* That his private Autho-rity is preferable to the general Senfe of all Ages and Countries, and fufficient to fet afide the *Verdict* of the Ancient and Modern Church.

Secondly, The *Stage*, in the Bifhop's time, was much more inoffenfive than it has been fince; the *indecencies* were not fo rank, nor the fallies of Prophanenefs fo frequent and hideous. That Matter of Fact ftands thus, is evident from the printed *Plays* of *Shake-fpear,*

[d] Serm. ad Pop. 4.
p. 252.
Defence of Plays,
p. 137.

[e] Ibid.

fpear and *Ben Johnfon*, of *Beaumont* and
Fletcher. 'Tis true, even this Entertainment, though comparatively clean, is oftentimes too lufcious and exceptionable. Farther; the Bifhop in all likelyhood, never
troubled himfelf to ftudy the *Stage*, and examine their Performances : He only thought
it poffible to ftand clear of Mifchief, and
make an inoffenfive *Play*. Upon this general Idea, he gives fomewhat of his Opinion, and draws towards a Refolution : But
even here he appears cold and difenclin'd,
and comes fhort of a ftate of Neutrality.
The Doctor confeffes, the Bifhop *does not
pretend to recommend the Calling of a Player*
‘ *Ib. p.136. as eligible* ᶠ. Right : All the favour he allows, is only *not abfolutely to condemn it.*
But does it follow from hence, that the Bifhop would have lent his Countenance to
the Licence and Immorality of the Modern
Stage ? Would he have fettled their Confciences in Smut and Profanenefs, and given
them his Bleffing to debauch the Nation ?
Can we imagine the Judgment and Piety of
this Prelate, could be fo far furpriz'd, as to
furnifh them with his Authority for fuch
wretched purpofes ? Arm them with the
ftrength of his Character, to drive over Decency and Shame ? To *read* upon a putri-
fied Carcafs, and fhew Nature, to the affront
of Religion. That this is the practice of the
Stage,

Stage, I have prov'd to a demonſtration. Now if Biſhop *Sanderſon* does not allow this Liberty, to what purpoſe is his Teſtimony brought?

To go ſomewhat lower: Is it likely the Biſhop's caſuiſtry would indulge even the Doctor's latitude, and come forward to his Plan of Reformation? That is, permit Proſtitutes and Bawds to make their Character in rank Language ; Atheiſts ſwear and blaſpheme, to let the *Audience* know what they are, and encourage the cutting of Throats, upon pretended Points of Honour? All this ſcandalous practice the Doctor pleads for, provided there is but Diſcipline at the end on't. But does this compaſs of Liberty agree with the Biſhop's Character? Or do we find ſuch looſe Reſolutions in his Caſes of Conſcience? No: He has given us no occaſion to blaſt his Reputation in this manner, and draw ſuch a Blemiſh upon his Memory.

The Doctor therefore will be oblig'd to quit his Hold, and look out farther. I confeſs, if he could have carry'd off a *Miter*, and made the *Pulpit* deſert to the *Stage*, tho' the Cauſe could not have been gain'd, there would have been ſomething of Exploit in it.

The Doctor now comes forward to the *Fathers*, endeavours to make their Teſtimony inoffenſive, and turn off the Point of their Satyr from the *Engliſh* Stage.

The

The force of his Argument lies in three Confiderations ; the firft of which is drawn from the Character of the Perfons: And here he very fairly tells us, *They were all Men of great Learning, and extraordinary Sanctity. —On whom God Almighty, in Favour, in Pity and Compaffion to his diftrefs'd Church, pour'd down more than ordinary Bleffings, and a larger portion of his Grace : Men in fhort, that by a long and affiduous Study, and conftant practice of Piety, defervedly rais'd themfelves above the common level of Mankind, and have ever fince been honour'd and diftinguifh'd by all fucceeding Ages, as the Fathers of the Church* ⸸.

⸸ Ib. p.146, 147.

Now by this commendation, which is no more than their due, one would think the Authority of the *Fathers* fhould be next to infallible: What may we not expect from the direction of fuch Perfons? Where Nature is improv'd to the utmoft, and unufually enlighten'd from *above?* Where there's no Mutiny of Paffions, no Secular Intereft, no overbalance of Pleafure to miflead the Judgment? Who would imagine fuch Men as thefe fhould be fo infignificant, nay fo dangerous in their Advice? Does the odds of their Underftanding, and the impartiality of their Temper, difable their Character, and make their word go for nothing? Are they blinded with too much Light, and perfectly overlay'd lay'd with Virtue and Senfe? 'Tis fomewhat difficult to clear the matter, and account for the Myftery upon thefe Principles. Yet fo it is, if we believe the Doctor, and therefore he muft have a care not to ftand to the Umperage of thefe antiquated Guides : For to practife up to their Maxims, as this Gentleman continues, *would certainly do more hurt than good, and make perhaps fome Atheifts, and a great many Hypocrites* [h]. To do the Doctor right, he grants the Doctrine of the *Fathers* was feafonable when they wrote ; but now their prefcriptions, like old Drugs, have loft their Force, and fignifie nothing. I grant the Sun has rifen, and the Moon chang'd a great many times fince the *Fathers* were living ; but for all that, Chriftianity, and Mankind, are juft the fame ftill. Neither the Malice of the Devil, the Punifhment of Vice, or the Rewards of Virtue, are a jot alter'd : Why then fhould we prefs for new Liberty, and go lefs in our circumfpection than former Ages? If the Rule muft bend to Practice, Principles be govern'd by Humour, and the Laws give way in proportion to the degeneracy of the Times: If this is the true expedient, to what a miferable declenfion in Morals muft we fink at laft? The confequence of this Cafuiftry will *difpenfe* with the *Bible*, and make the Apoftles *Writings* as little fignificant as thofe of the *Fathers*.

Farther ;

[h] *Idem, P. 148. Ibid.*

Farther ; That the Deſtruction of *Hea-thenifm*, and the Reſpit from Perſecution, does not alter the meaſure of Duty in this caſe, I have prov'd in my ſecond Defence of the *Short View* [i], &c. and thither I refer the Doctor. In this *Tract*, his *third obſervable* drawn from the *Nature of thofe Plays the Fathers wrote againſt* [k], is likewiſe examin'd, and ſhewn unſerviceable to his purpoſe.

His next effort is to encourage the Duels of the *Stage*, and keep Quarrels and murthering in Countenance [l]. Now in my Opinion, he ſhould have anſwer'd my Reaſons againſt this Cuſtom [m], before he had given it a Licence, and brought it within the Privilege of his *Reformation*.

And now having done with the Doctor's *Book*, I would gladly prevail with him to conſider, that the Defence of the *Play-Houfe* is an impracticable undertaking. 'Tis to no purpoſe to go about to rub out the colours of Virtue and Vice ; Ribaldry and Profaneneſs will ne're paſs undiſcover'd in a Chriſtian Country. The ſubject is much too coarſe to be overcaſt with Sophiſtry and Diſtinctions : All attempts of this kind lie open to miſcarriage and diſappointment : For by endeavouring to perplex the Cauſe, and darken the evidence of Truth, a Man is oftentimes ſmother'd in his own Smoak, and raiſes a Miſt to loſe himſelf in.

F I N I S.

[i] P. 2, 3, 12, 14.

[k] *Defence of Plays,* p. 152.

[l] *Idem,* p. 156.

[m] *View,* &c. p. 283, 284. *Second Defence,* p. 59, 60.

BOOKS printed for RICHARD SARE and GEORGE STRAHAN.

A Short View of the Profaneneſs and Immorality of the *Engliſh* Stage ; with the ſenſe of Antiquity upon this Argument: 8°. price 3 s. 6 d.

A Defence of the ſhort View of the Profaneneſs and Immorality of the *Engliſh* Stage, *&c.* being a Reply to Mr. *Congreve's* Amendments, *&c.* 8°. price 18 d.

A ſecond Defence of the ſhort View, *&c.* in Anſwer to a Book, entituled, *The Ancient and Modern Stages vindicated*, 8°. price 1 s. 6 d.

The Emperor *M. Antoninus* his Converſation with himſelf ; together with the preliminary Diſcourſe of the Learned *Gataker.* As alſo the Emperor's Life, written by *M. D'Acier*, and ſupported by the Authorities collected by Dr. *Stanhope.* To which is added, the Mythological Picture of *Cebes* the *Theban.* Tranſlated into *Engliſh* from their reſpective Originals, 8°. price 5 s.

Eſſays upon ſeveral Moral Subjects ; in Two Parts. The Fifth Edition, 8°. price 5 s.

A Diſſuaſive from the *Play-houſe* ; price 3 d.
Theſe ſix by the Reverend Mr. Collier.

A Practical Diſcourſe concerning Swearing, eſpecially in the two great Points of Perjury and common Swearing, 8°. price 1 s. 6 d.

The Principles of the Chriſtian Religion, explain'd in a Brief Commentary on the Church Catechiſm, 8°. price 2 s.

The Church of *Rome* no Guide in Matters of Faith, in anſwer to a Letter from a Nephew to his Uncle, containing his Reaſons why he became a Roman Catholick, and why he now declines any farther Diſputes about Matters of Religion. 8°. price 6 d.
Theſe 3 by Dr. Wake, Lord Biſhop of Lincoln.

EPictetus's Morals, with *Simplicius's* Comment, done into *Engliſh.* The Third Edition : With the Addition of the Life of *Epictetus*, 8°. price 5 s.

Parſons his Chriſtian Directory ; being a Treatiſe of Holy Reſolution, in Two Parts ; purged from all Errors, and put into modern *Engliſh.* And now made publick for the Inſtruction of the Ignorant, Conviction of Unbelievers, Awakening and Reclaiming the Vicious, and for Confirming Religious Perſons in their good Purpoſes, 8°. price 5 s.

The Chriſtian Pattern, or a Treatiſe of the Imitation of Jeſus Chriſt ; in Four Books. Written originally in *Latin* by
Thomas

Thomas à Kempis. To which are added Meditations and Prayers for Sick Persons, in 8°. with Cuts, price 5 s. And also in 12°. price 2 s.

The Truth and Excellence of the Christian Religion asserted, against Jews, Infidels, and Hereticks; in Sixteen Sermons preach'd at the Cathedral Church of St. *Paul*, in the Years, 1701, 1702, being the Lectures founded by the Hon. R. *Boyle*, 4°. price bound 9 s.

A Paraphrase and Comment upon the Epistles and Gospels, appointed to be used by the Church of *England*, on all *Sundays* and *Holydays* throughout the Year. Designed to excite Devotion, and promote the Knowledge and Practice of sincere Piety and Vertue; in Four Volumes. The 1st, 2d, and 3d Volumes, already printed, and the 4th in the Press.

These Five by Dr. Stanhope, *Dean of* Canterbury.

THE Works of *Flavius Josephus*, translated into *English*. Folio.

Fables of *Æsop*, and other eminent *Mythologists*, with Morals and Reflections. 8°.

Fables and Stories moralized; being a Second Part of the Fables of *Æsop*, and other eminent *Mythologists*. 8°.

Twenty two select Colloquies out of *Erasmus Roterodamus*; pleasantly representing several superstitious Levities that were crept into the Church of *Rome* in his Days. 8°. pr. 2 s. 6 d.

Quevedo's Visions; the Ninth Edition, 8°. price 2 s. 6 d.

These Five by Sir Roger L'Estrange.

THE Essay towards a Proposal for Catholick Communion, &c. lately published by a (pretended) Minister of the Church of *England*; printed at large, and answered Chapter by Chapter. By *N. Spinkes*, a Presbyter of the Church of *England*, 8°. price 4 s.

AN Answer to all the Excuses and Pretences that Men ordinarily make for their not coming to the Holy Communion. To which is added, a Brief Account of the End and Design of the Holy Communion; the obligation to receive it; the way to prepare for it. And the Behaviour of our selves, both at, and after it, &c. Price 3 d. or 20 s. per 100.

Plain Instructions for the Young and Ignorant; compriz'd in a short and easie Exposition of the Church Catechism. Adapted to the Understanding and Memory of the meanest Capacity. Price 3 d. or 20 s. per 100.

These Two by the same Author.

THE Reasonableness and Certainty of the Christian Religion. In Two Volumes. The former comprehending what was thought necessary for the Proof thereof. The latter containing Discourses upon such Subjects as are thought most liable to Objections. By *Robert Jenkin*, late Fellow of St. *John's* College in *Cambridge*.